You can't get lower than this

Publications by the Author

'Lucky Lad – Memories of the Upper Dearne Valley' ISBN 978-0-9555978-0-0	2007

Local and Family History Articles:

'Thurstonland Township Parish Chest Records'	2000
'A Population Study of the Upper Dearne Valley from Census Returns 1801-1841'	2002
'Employment Statistics and Occupations in the Upper Dearne Valley from 1841 Census'	2002
'Distractions'	2004
'Stamp Duty Act 1793 – A Case Study'	2009
'The Crigglestone Colliery Explosion – A Family's Triple Tragedy'	2010
'James Brown – Huddersfield's Victorian Luthier'	2012
'Scandal in the Upper Dearne Valley'	2013
'A Remarkable Centenarian'	2016

ISBN 978-0-9555978-1-7

9 780955 597817

You can't get lower than this

NOTES FROM A VETERAN ORCHESTRAL BASSIST

EDWARD G HELLEWELL

Published September 2016.

Graig Press
80 Cefn Graig, Rhiwbina, Cardiff, CF14 6JZ.
email: graigpress@virginmedia.com

Design & Print by:
AA Media
The Coach House, Dock Street, Penarth, CF64 2LA.
Tel: 029 2000 3846
email: sales@aamedia.co.uk

ISBN 978-0-9555978-1-7

CONTENTS

Acknowledgements

With love and heartfelt thanks to Angela for encouragement and advice and for taking me through the difficult times during the preparation of this book.

To Mary Dewey my sincere thanks for undertaking the unenviable task of correcting my punctuation, grammar and spelling at the proof reading stage.

Dedicated to amateur musicians everywhere
especially members of the orchestral bass section and
to my wonderful granddaughters
Mari, Alice, Jane, Lily, Eve, Katherine, Amelia and Miranda

PREFACE

An undistinguished career, by professional standards at least, has been my lot in a music making career commencing in the days of blackout and rationing towards the end of the Second World War. Nevertheless, it has been a great privilege for me to participate in all manner of ensembles which has given me great satisfaction and, above all else, has been tremendous fun.

I am able to look back over substantially more than two thousand performances. Firstly with the violin as a young boy in an orchestra and as a soloist. Secondly as a teenager with the trombone in brass bands, dance bands, jazz bands, and later in orchestras and also as a soloist. I was finally captured and captivated by the king of orchestral instruments, the double bass. My bass playing career stretches back some 63 years, when as a dance band trombonist, I was taught the rudiments of pizzicato bass by my rhythm section colleague, bassist Gilbert Pell. This early introduction to the mysteries of bass playing proved something of a false start, since Gilbert played on an old 3 string bass tuned in fifths. It was only a little time later on renewing my acquaintance on a borrowed instrument that I suddenly discovered basses usually had 4 strings but more importantly, they were tuned in fourths.

It is as an amateur that I've played throughout my career, although that is not to say I've never been paid for a performance. Indeed, I can claim to have turned professional at the age of 11 when I joined a 'pit' band run by my fiddle teacher, which accompanied local amateur operatic society shows. As a dance band trombonist I was paid a fee for every gig, but this could never have supported me. However, the prospect of turning full time professional with the bass never appealed to me, but more importantly I simply wasn't good enough. I never had the advantage of conservatoire training, actually being essentially self-taught. In any case, as the late great French Horn player Alan Civil remarked of playing 2nd or 4th horn parts, *"there's no money in low notes."* That was also my conclusion of being a professional rank and file orchestral bass player.

The purpose of this book is to provide the music lover, and perhaps the non-committed as well, with a light hearted insight into amateur instrumental music making through my own varied experiences and in so doing perform a little education along the way. Since the book is mainly about the amateur music scene, the potential for 'cock-ups' in these ensembles is enormous – although that does not imply that the professionals get it right every time!

Of all the orchestral instruments, the double bass is probably the least well known, despite being the largest and on prominent display on the concert hall platform. Bass players, certainly of my age having stayed with it for so long, are nothing if not enthusiasts, and want to tell everyone what a marvellous instrument it is. So this book also provides the opportunity for a further bit of education and publicity for the double bass, known in the trade simply as a bass.

The book, however, is not an exhaustive treatise on the bass, but rather a description of certain aspects and the playing of it. For those interested in pursuing their knowledge of the instrument, the definitive work I would recommend is:
'A New History of the Double Bass' by Paul Brun, ISBN 2-9514461-0-1

An informative and highly readable, but less extensive book that I would suggest is:
'About the Double Bass – a player's guide' by Peter Tyler, ISBN 978-0-956981.

The names of individuals mentioned in the text are not fictitious and if I have caused embarrassment then I apologise unreservedly. To offend or cause embarrassment has never been my intention. Recalling events in a musical career stretching back over 70 years certainly tests the memory banks, and it is always possible I've made the odd mistake with a name, a date, a place or other detail. Any errors if they occur are entirely my responsibility.

Instrumentalists have a hard time of it. Relentless hours of practice, not only when learning the instrument but also slogging away in solitude as a more advanced player, attempting to perfect a few tricky passages. Realising, after all, that one's technique simply isn't good enough to cope with the technical demands of a few fiendish bars of music, can be disheartening to say the least.

Turning out in the pouring rain on a dark winter's night to attend a rehearsal in a cold and draughty church hall is never an attractive proposition. The appealing alternative of a cosy night in front of the TV with a glass of wine in hand is hard to resist. It's no wonder that so many fall by the wayside. Yet, for those prepared to dedicate a huge chunk of their lives to mastering their chosen instrument the rewards are tremendous. For the relative few who last the course and finally make it into the ranks of a good amateur orchestra, that is the pinnacle of achievement. Is all the effort worth it? You bet!

'Music expresses that which cannot be said and on which it is impossible to be silent'

- Victor Hugo

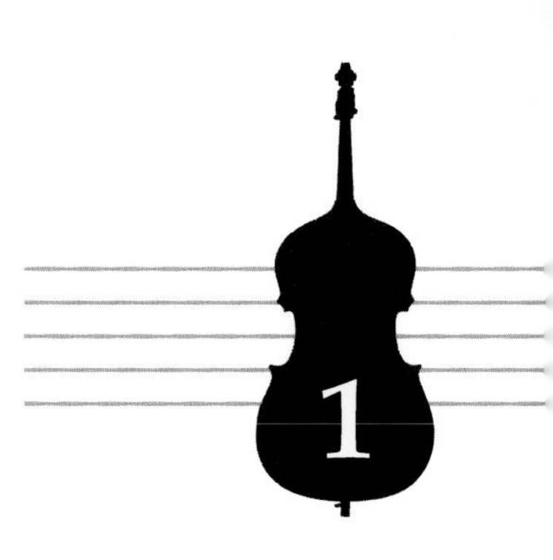

Fiddle First

Most amateur players today who make it into a decent standard adult orchestra have followed the direct route of school orchestra, various grades of youth orchestra followed by university or college orchestra. In contrast, my arrival at that stage in my musical career followed a circuitous and somewhat unusual sequence. What's more, before the double bass and I were to become lifelong orchestral companions, I had played two other instruments with varying degrees of success in orchestras, as well as a variety of other musical ensembles.

My orchestral adventures began in the days of blackout and rationing towards the end of the 2nd World War. As a short-trousered 9 year old I sat at the back of the 2nd violins in a small local orchestra playing in the Memorial Hall, Denby Dale the next village to my home. I count myself fortunate indeed to have been born and brought up in the Upper Dearne Valley, situated in the foothills of the Southwest Yorkshire Pennines. Despite being a rough and tumble working class area, the district had a remarkable thriving musical tradition with choirs, amateur operatic societies and especially brass bands. Brass bands were the dominant musical force and amazingly, there were 11 within a 5 mile radius of my home.

The district's sole 'permanent' orchestra was organised and conducted by Milton Beever, a schoolteacher in Barnsley and a keen amateur cellist. I have great respect for Milton, since he was a kind, sympathetic man who, unlike several other conductors I've encountered in my long musical career, never attempted to demonstrate how clever he was or to show up a player who simply *'could not get it right'*. The orchestra was ably led by Willie Kaye, my fiddle teacher. Most members if not all, were adults, and I was by far the youngest. I wasn't a particularly advanced player, but I owed my inclusion entirely to Willie, who thought I was just about competent enough to play the easier bits, and sensible enough *'leave off'* when the inevitable forest of black notes appeared so that I didn't mess things up. I don't remember much about that first concert other than we played Haydn's Surprise Symphony, and that my chair suffered from a dreadful squeak.

My debut as an orchestra professional occurred a couple of years later when Willie asked me if I'd like to join his *'pit band'* which accompanied local amateur operatic society shows and pantomimes. Willie was the local *'fixer'*. At a fee of between £1 and 30 shillings (£1.50) for a band call, 4 week nights, Saturday evening and the occasional Saturday matinee, how could I refuse? The money was just too good to miss, but more than that, it was good fun. To look the part, Mum bought me a new white shirt, a natty black bow tie and a pair of short black trousers. I don't remember many of the personnel except Willie who led, Victor Senior my second fiddle desk partner, and the cellist Albion Burt from Emley, a village situated about 3 miles from my home. Come rain or shine, Albion always arrived at the venue in a cloud of blue smoke on an ancient 2 stroke motorbike, with the cello strapped to his back. Sadly, Albion met his end on that motorbike several years later.

The standard of these amateur shows was very high indeed, but that's not surprising given the immense amount of rehearsal time by the cast, ably supported by a minor army of set designers, scenery painters, costume ladies, lighting men, carpenters and many others who were involved. The pianists were always provided by the society, since these brave souls had slogged through week after week of rehearsals during which time the principals and chorus painstakingly learnt the show's songs. One of the best, and friendliest to me, was Miss Winnie Firth, later Mrs Winnie Adamski, who was Scissett Amateur Operatic Society's accompanist in my home village. The musical director, who also conducted the performances came from each of the societies. In my limited experience, the outstanding people were Stephen Wray at Scissett and Mrs Pobjoy at Emley. The latter was a brilliant musician, who also happened to be the Rector's wife. Her talents extended to writing both the script and the music for many of her productions. For me the most memorable show was Scissett's 1949 production of The Boyfriend, the lead being taken by a pretty teenager, Barbara Gill, with whom I instantly fell in love. Some 10 years later, I married her cousin.

'Sings' were another musical event in which I participated with the violin and, in later years with the trombone and eventually with the bass. These were open-air vocal gatherings very popular in the area around Barnsley and Huddersfield. These took place on the afternoon of the respective villages' Feast Sunday. An ad-hoc choir raised from the local churches and chapels often numbering a hundred or so voices, sang well-loved hymns and oratorio choruses with the spectators joining in. The singers were elevated on a temporary tiered wooden stage with the orchestra arrayed in front at ground level. Since there was no control on the capability of the orchestral players, the number who turned up, nor the instrumental balance, some pretty weird sounds emanated from these ad-hoc ensembles. Almost invariably the choruses were *Hallelujah, And the Glory, Worthy is the Lamb* from Handel's Messiah, with the *Gloria* from Mozart's 12th Mass and Haydn's The Heavens are Telling receiving an occasional airing. The nearest equivalent I'm aware of, but minus the oratorio choruses, is the Gymanfa Ganu in Wales.

Well, how did I come to be playing violin in the first instance? Nowadays, children often have the opportunity to try an instrument in school and if they like it then pester their parents to purchase one. There was no possibility in my day for school to provide an instrument, but remarkably I didn't have to pester Mum and Dad. Both were music lovers and keen amateur pianists, so they presumably thought I would be inclined to music. For some unknown reason they concluded that I should perhaps branch out with an instrument other than the piano. Quite out of the blue, a mysterious long box wrapped up in brown paper materialised on my 7th birthday. Imagining this to be a Hornby clockwork train set, the true desire of my heart, I ripped the paper off to reveal a well-worn leatherette covered case. My disappointment was complete when, upon opening the case, there was no shiny engine, trucks and rails but a reddish brown violin. I hardly knew what the thing was and I'd certainly never seen one at such close quarters, let alone handled one. It transpired that my Dad had purchased the violin for £5 from Charlie Lockwood who lived in Emley. £5 doesn't sound much these days, but over 70 years ago I suppose it was a fair price for a German Markneukirchen copy of a double purfled Italian Maggini. For sentimental reasons, I still have this fiddle sitting on the top of my piano today.

The question of lessons then became a hot topic of discussion and Willie, who at that time was living in Kirkburton some 6 miles from home, agreed to weekly lessons at 2 shillings (20p) a time. Today, even allowing for inflation, that sounds a real bargain for his undoubted expertise and an hour and a half of his time. Willie was a young-looking, tall, debonair man with slicked down black hair with a parting, typical of the time. He had been a pupil of Laurence Turner, originally from Huddersfield, who led the Halle with great distinction for many years – I believe Willie also had a spell with the Halle. Incidentally, Turner was a pupil of the more famous Huddersfield teacher Arthur Willie Kaye (no relation to my teacher) who in turn had been a pupil of the world-renowned Czech violinist, Sevcik, notorious amongst generations of violin students for his fiendish bowing studies. With such a distinguished pedigree I really should have made something of the violin, however that was not to be.

My first lesson was on 21st March 1943. I can even remember Willie telling me at the start of the lesson that I would always remember the date, since it was the first day of Spring. A teacher's style can have an enormous influence on the development of a pupil and in this respect I was very fortunate. I liked Willie, for he taught by example and was quick to praise a good effort. On the other hand he was a 'stickler' for accuracy, and quick to reproach if he thought I'd shirked practice – he claimed he could always detect immediately if I'd missed out on that daily task. After his explanation and my initial attempts, Willie always played the exercises and pieces he'd set for the next week, simply to reinforce what I was aiming at. During the last few minutes, as a relaxation and encouragement for me, he always played from memory something more advanced, such as excerpts from concertos, sonatas or some *'showy'* piece of Kreisler or Paganini. I simply loved these impromptu performances and I looked forward to the day when hopefully, I'd be able to emulate him. In the main I did practice diligently, and soon I reached the end of my fairly thick tutor book (the name now escapes me and the book is sadly missing!). I then moved on to several books crammed with nothing but graded exercises, including the famous studies of Kayser and the afore mention Sevcik. These were designed to develop a decent technique. In addition we worked on solos, including easier excerpts from concertos and sonatas to encourage musicality, phrasing, rubato, interpretation and the like.

Whilst still in junior school I was invited to play solos in concerts throughout the district. These were variety concerts purely for entertainment and consequently none too highbrow. My contribution for example, could be sandwiched between a dialect recitation of *Albert and the Lion*, and a vocalist giving a rendition of *The Lost Chord*. In such concerts *'serious'* fiddle pieces were out of the question, and I relied on favourites such as

Staendchen, made famous by the popular violinist Albert Sandler, and Roses from the South. To put it mildly pianos in village, church and chapel halls were of variable quality and Mum who accompanied me often had to contend with sticking keys and squeaky pedals. At that stage of my musical career I never worried about standing on the platform performing in front of an audience of perhaps a couple of hundred people, and I certainly derived a great deal of pleasure from playing these concerts.

In stark contrast I really detested the competitive side of violin playing, although to please Mum, Dad and Willie I did submit to the ordeal. For competition work it was decided that I ought to have a better sounding violin. In recent years I've discovered that the one I then acquired was old English, variously dated between 1780 and 1840. Again, for sentimental reasons I've retained this instrument. There were several musical festivals at Leeds, Bradford, Keighley, Holmfirth, and the local Mrs Sunderland at Huddersfield, all with age group classes for violin. I never won any of the events, but usually came in the top 10 of 30 plus entrants – I even made it into the top 3 on occasion. A notable fellow competitor was Rodney Friend who is now recognised internationally as one of the outstanding English born violinists. He went on to carve out a distinguished solo career and also lead several of the world's great orchestras including the BBC Symphony, the London Symphony, the London Philharmonic, the New York Philharmonic and the English Chamber Orchestra. At a young age he displayed an awesome talent, and needless to say I can't recall Rodney ever being beaten. He always performed without music and I remember thinking at the time what a marvellous memory he must have. It was only later I realised that this feat probably reflected the sheer volume of practice he'd put into each piece. The immense amount of preparation and practice I had to invest in the various test pieces, seemed out of all proportion to the enjoyment I actually derived from playing them, and many weren't all that tuneful either. Performing in front of an eagle-eyed adjudicator and a super-critical audience of fellow competitors, their parents and teachers, was a nerve racking experience to say the least.

Although by the age of 14 I had attained a decent standard my interest in the violin had waned considerably, and consequently I lacked the enthusiasm for diligent practice necessary to reach a higher level or indeed maintain the standard I had already achieved. It gradually dawned on me that violins hadn't much street cred in a rough and tumble mining and textile district. As an added distraction, I was becoming interested in the hugely popular big dance bands and also the smaller traditional jazz bands. Music of the former was being broadcast frequently on the radio, some bands having their own half-hour weekly slot. In neither of these combinations was there a place for a violin.

My fiddle playing career was ended suddenly by one competition in which I was placed 30 something – the only time I'd ever had such a lowly result. The test piece was quite a difficult one and in disgust I threw the music away immediately afterwards. Today I can't even remember the title. Cruelly, the first note was a harmonic D, which due to nerves many of the competitors failed to produce. I thought I had given a decent performance and whilst waiting for the results several in the audience complimented me. The adjudicator thought differently. His written remarks concentrated entirely on what he considered to be a faulty technique – a dropped left wrist and an arcing bow stroke. He made not the slightest mention of my actual performance and what I sounded like. With the benefit of years of hindsight, I came to realise my basic technique could have been much better and with that handicap I had possibly reached the limit of my playing ability. Perhaps the adjudicator knew this and was being cruel to be kind.

However, I resolved there and then to make a complete break from the violin after 7 years of daily practice, apart from the last 12 months or so when I did lapse. When I announced that I was terminating my fiddling career immediately, Mum, Dad and Willie naturally, were disappointed. Nevertheless, they took it with good grace and to their credit didn't attempt to persuade me otherwise. For their calm reaction I was much relieved since I had feared that Dad, who had a short fuse temper, would be likely to despatch at least a few sharp words in my direction.

2

Blown Away By The Brass

Despite music being part of my life for so long, it came as something of a relief to be free of the burden of daily practice and quite honestly, I felt a sense of freedom. Truth to tell I missed violin playing not a jot. Musically, for several months I did absolutely nothing. Serendipity put an end to that and set me off on what turned out to be one of the most enjoyable stages of my musical adventures. One evening I just happened to call round to see a cornet playing friend, John Hallas. His father George fortunately for me was sitting in the living room reading the newspaper. George was the conductor of Clayton West Brass Band. I already knew George from his occasional appearances playing trumpet in Willie Kaye's 'pit' band. He'd heard that I'd stopped fiddling and offered me the opportunity to try an old B flat tenor trombone which had been lying around in the band room for years.

I'd never given a thought to playing a brass instrument, but I suddenly felt excited at the prospect of a new musical challenge and I readily agreed to at least give it a try. George then arranged for Albert Wood the band's solo trombone player to teach me. The instrument on offer, an old small bore Boosey trombone, really was past its best. These instruments were often called 'pea-shooters' on account of the small bore. I remember well my first evening's visit to Albert's house to make an acquaintance with my instrument and have my first lesson. The evening got off to a shaky start for, on pulling the instrument out of its old leather case, the slide was found to be broken. Albert was totally non-plussed and with the aid of a petrol blowlamp, he skilfully soldered the inner slide to the cross stay. The trombone was now just about usable, but needless to say the slide action was dreadful and no amount of different lubricant concoctions would improve it.

Several months of free private lessons from Albert provided some mastery of the blowing and slide positions in both the treble and tenor clefs. It sounds pretty horrendous to have to learn the slide positions in two clefs, but in the brass band world this isn't as difficult as it sounds. The simple trick of knocking off 2 flats or, if there weren't enough flats, adding 2 sharps, allows the tenor clef to be read as the treble clef. From my fiddle playing days I could read music pretty well so that aspect didn't present any problems and it was therefore mainly a matter of building up a decent embouchure and lip stamina, which only time and practice can do. Before too long, a reshuffle took place in the band and the 2nd trombone chair became vacant. Solo trombonist Albert thought I was capable of filling it and so I joined him and bass trombonist, Phillip Hallas, George's brother, as a full band member. I was delighted to find that a much better small bore Boosey trombone went with the position.

Clayton West band room was a cosy wooden hut which in winter, had the luxury of a free-standing coke stove. Arrayed around the walls were photos of the bands of old, with many of the ancient players looking like proper desperados sporting an eclectic range of moustaches. I can't remember the first piece I ever played in rehearsal, but to this day I can still feel the thrill of being washed over by the massive sound of a full band at double forte. In modern day parlance I was literally *'blown away'*.

Joining that particular band was an amazing piece of luck. The bandsmen taught me such a lot, not just about music but also about life. I had now moved into an adult world and my whole boyish attitude to life changed. I wanted to succeed as a trombone player and was prepared to work very hard to achieve that goal. I now became part of a wonderfully diverse group of players who took me under their wing. The players were all working class men, grafting hard in manual jobs. The 'corner men' of the band had a variety of jobs. Principal cornet Arthur Exley and solo euphonium Ned Mosley, were foundrymen at Addy's Foundry in Clayton West. Solo horn Alf Haigh worked underground at Clayton West's Park Mill colliery, soprano cornet Dennis Tucker was an overlooker at the village's Beanland's textile mill, and solo trombone Albert Wood, was a painter and decorator. Educationally, they had never had much of a chance in life, yet they were intelligent people with wide ranges of interest. Despite their lack of formal academic qualifications, they encouraged me to take up technical studies when I started work. As a grammar school boy I'd led something of a sheltered life, never having come into really close contact with working men. In truth, I was taken aback by their talents and willingness to pass on their hard-earned knowledge and experience to me. First and foremost they were keen, skilled musicians and, for me a great inspiration.

George Hallas, the band's conductor was an excellent cornet player, who had played with Brighouse & Rastrick Band, and I believe also the CWS Band in Manchester. George was quietly spoken in rehearsal but nevertheless authoritative, and he knew precisely the musical interpretation he wanted. I'll be eternally grateful for the training and advice I received from him. My best mate in the band was his brother, bass trombone colleague Phillip Hallas. Phillip had served in the Kings Own Yorkshire Light Infantry in the 2nd War and had endured incredible hardship and unspeakable horrors fighting the Japanese in the jungles of Burma in both campaigns. Phillip was a painter and decorator by trade, while only 17 years older than I was, he initially looked after me, almost like a son. On band engagements we were pretty much inseparable, and on the long coach journeys we always sat next to each other and chatted the hours away.

Playing in the band opened up a whole new vista of musical experience and introduced me to some of the great classical compositions, as well as many original brass band pieces. In addition to the big name composers, I also came to know many of classical music's lesser-known ones such as Balfe, Wallace, Reissiger, Boildieu and Auber – names hardly known today and whose tuneful compositions are now rarely heard. I'd never played a march before, but soon found myself thrilled to be belting out the 'bass solos' of such favourites as Slaidburn, BB&CF, Punchinello, Avondale and many others. From the orchestral repertoire I was excited by the arrangements of overtures with Poet and Peasant, The Caliph of Baghdad, Morning, Noon and Night, Tancredi, Light Cavalry and The Mill on the Cliff being particular favourites. At that time, the band world relied heavily on arrangements of the classics and of selections from operas and operettas. From my very early days in banding, I remember playing an arrangement of Dvorak's symphony From the New World, and selections from Wallace's Maritana and Balfe's The Bohemian Girl. Special to me was William Rimmer's fantasia on Rule Britannia, a stirring piece but with a contrasting quiet trombone trio which was a great joy to play. I'm delighted that this work has been revived and recorded in recent years by the Fodens Courtois band. The engagements the band undertook were concerts in churches and chapels, open-air performances in the parks (Greenhead Huddersfield, Wilthorpe Barnsley, Normanton etc) and leading parades and marches. The band hadn't entered brass band contests for many years probably the last one was pre-WWII.

Although by no means mediocre, conductor George decided that the best way to improve our playing standard was through the contest arena. It was in the early 1950's that bands were beginning to decline in popularity. Locally, both Denby and Denby Dale bands folded around this time through lack of players. We were fortunate to enlist some very good players from Denby Dale, which pre–war had an excellent record and had even done wireless broadcasts. Edwin Cunningham on tenor horn and his father Raymond on Bflat bass, Clifford Horsely on cornet and an excellent trombonist Alan Thomas, joined within a short time. The latter player released Albert Wood to move from solo trombone to Eflat bass. The band had always rehearsed twice a week on Tuesday and Friday evenings and now, because of our serious commitment to contesting, a third rehearsal was scheduled for Sunday afternoons.

Since the band had no recent track record we were automatically placed in the lowest (4th section) of the Daily Herald championship structure. Our first outing was to the North East Region contest at Huddersfield Town Hall, the test piece being an original band work Wayside Scenes, by J.A. Greenwood. I don't remember much about the piece except it had a trombone trio about half way through. 23 bands entered and we were placed a creditable 5th with 186 points, the winners being Leeds City who scored 194 points. I stayed on to hear the 2nd section contest in the evening with 13 bands taking part. The winners were Hade Edge, with Royston New Monkton Colliery placed second and local band Skelmanthorpe, fourth. Later in my career I freelanced with these particular bands. This contest was the first time I had met up with players from other bands and I was immediately struck by their friendliness, despite the intense rivalry on the competition platform. I felt immensely proud to be part of such a wonderful movement. Our first win playing an arrangement of Beethoven's Mignon, was several weeks later in May at the Belle Vue Spring contest.

The band continued to perform well in contests and I have a vivid memory of playing the next year in the Daily Herald 3rd section at Leeds Town Hall, although on that occasion we were unplaced. There I met a charming girl Grace Dinsdale, who was principal cornet with the York Railway Institute Band. It was very rare in those days to have girls in bands, let alone one playing top cornet. Truth to tell, I was captivated by her. The evening contest for championship section bands included illustrious names such the YEWCO Works (this band contained some players from the world famous professional

St Hilda Colliery Band, which had disbanded in 1937), Crossley's Carpets, Butterfield's Tank Works, Markham Main Colliery, Brighouse & Rastrick, Carlton Main Frickley Colliery and Leeds Model. Some years later I had the privilege to freelance with the latter three bands. However, as a young lad on that contest day I was absolutely overawed by the musicality and sheer technical brilliance of all the champion section bands. For me it was a tremendous inspiration to knuckle down to some determined practice.

As so often down the years the winner on that occasion, was Black Dyke Mills, regarded by many for their consistency as the outstanding band of all time. Because of their eminent position they were able to attract the very best players on all instruments and, especially a distinguished series of solo cornet players dating back to the Victorian era. The list of the latter includes virtuosi such as Alexander Owen, John Paley, Cyres Jackson, Harold Pinches, Harold Jackson and Owen Bottomley. Their principal cornet that day was the remarkable Willie Lang.

Willie Lang was brought up in Norland, a hamlet to the south west of Halifax, and as he once remarked, there was nothing else to do there other than practice. He joined Black Dyke Mills at the age of 16 as deputy to principal cornet, Harold Jackson, a position to which he was appointed a year later. A stonemason by training and trade, he was called up for military service and served as a tank driver at the Battle of Alamein. There is a story that he drove his tank for an unbroken 24 hours in the lead up to the battle, and throughout whistled the solo cornet part of the brass band test piece Life Divine. Willie survived the battle and years later compared playing in a symphony orchestra to war; most of the time you're bored to tears but occasionally you're frightened to death. He was well qualified to make that statement having moved into the orchestral world for a long professional career, first with the West Riding Orchestra, then as a member of the Halle, and finally with the London Symphony Orchestra. Incidentally, some 3 years or so after Willie left Black Dyke Mills band the brilliant Maurice Murphy was appointed solo cornet. He became a legend in his own lifetime in a long orchestral career culminating as principal trumpet in the LSO, with whom he performed his final concert at the remarkable age of 71.

Brass bands then had a reputation as hard drinking outfits. Some were like that, but drink had no place on the contest platform. Conductor George insisted on total abstinence until the band had played. This was more than mild torture if we'd been unlucky with the draw and had to wait hours before our turn to perform. However, the respect for George and the players' dedication was such that I can't ever remember anyone breaking the rule. After playing – well, that was a very different matter. I had my first drink shortly after I joined the band. Phillip bought it for me on condition I didn't tell my Dad. I did enjoy a beer or two and even the odd whisky from time to time. I vowed that because Mum and Dad had trusted me with a house key to let myself in, often in the small hours of the morning, I'd never return home seriously worse for wear. Mum and Dad must have realised that I had started drinking, well underage of course, but never passed comment.

From the band we also formed a trombone quartet, again for contest purposes. Alan Thomas played first trombone, I played second, Stuart Gill from Skelmanthorpe Band guested on third with Phillip Hallas bass trombone. Horn player Alf Haigh was the conductor and our speciality was Comrades in Arms. Quartet contests and solo slow melody contests were very popular then, and were often held in working men's clubs as Saturday evening entertainment. Our first successes were contests at Silkstone and Spring Vale clubs where we won hands down. The most serious and prestigious quartet contest was at Holmebridge. At that venue we never managed to beat a superb trombone quartet from Scotland's John Fauld's Works Band led by the talented player, George Gilmour. These quartet contests allowed any combination of 4 brass instruments, and some pretty unusual and, in many ways amusing outfits turned up – 4 basses, 4 horns, 2 cornets and 2 trombones for example, although the most popular choice was 2 cornets, horn and euphonium.

Although I was still playing second trombone at Clayton West, by now bands in higher sections were becoming interested in signing me, some offering the first trombone chair. I was sorely tempted to go, but a reshuffle in the band with Alan Thomas moving to euphonium allowed me to move up to solo trombone. I enjoyed the responsibility and for concerts I was expected to play either one or perhaps two solos. The 'flashy' numbers I chose were The Acrobat and The Joker whilst my slow melodies were Where'ere You Walk, Angels Guard Thee and Panis Angelicus.

I'd made good progress in the band without specialist tuition and several players suggested to my Dad that I would benefit from private lessons from a 'proper' trombone teacher. I'm not sure how it was arranged, but I was taken under Grenville Richmond's wing at Brighouse and Rastrick. Although Grenville was still in his 20's he had been solo trombone with this famous band for some years, having himself been a pupil of the respected teacher, Ernest Appleyard. I travelled every Saturday morning to have my lesson at Grenville's parent's house in Rastrick and looked forward eagerly to the experience. Grenville taught by example and with him I progressed by leaps and bounds. I enjoyed studying some of the classic trombone solos made famous by Arthur Pryor, who was referred to as The Paganni of the Trombone. He was principal trombonist with the famous Sousa band and is reputed to have played over 10,000 solo performances. My particular favourites were Loves Enchantment and variations on Blue Bells of Scotland. In fairness, these are quite difficult solos and I always felt very nervous when performing them in public. The second note of each is a sustained high brass band D (concert pitch C) which follows a terrifying octave leap upward. Once this had been successfully negotiated the blood pressure dropped a shade!!

After a while Greville thought I would perform well in slow melody contests. These events always drew large entries, with up to 40 in each class. Usually there was a junior class (with an upper age limit of 17? years), which often commenced as early as 1pm. After a break for tea the open section usually got under way at 6pm and often didn't finish until around 10pm, such were the number of entries. Cornet players were in the majority closely followed by those performing on horn and euphonium. Playing the trombone, at least I gave the unseen adjudicator a welcome change from listening to an almost unbroken stream of the popular favourites; The Holy City and The Lost Chord. For slow melody contests, the pieces I studied with Grenville were Nirvana and Lend Me Your Aid along with my particular favourite, Where'ere You Walk. In contrast to my dislike of violin competitions, I found these occasions very enjoyable and there was a friendly atmosphere amongst listeners and competitors alike. My best result was at Marsden in the Colne Valley where I won the junior event in the afternoon and on the same day came second in the evening's open event, both with Where'ere You Walk – I only wish I'd kept the adjudicator's remarks. A regular at these events was a young talented Eflat bass player from Slaithwaite band, Roland Atkinson, who always gave a polished performance of Asleep in the Deep. This piece written as a Basso Profundo vocal solo in 1896 by Petrie, is as its name suggests ideal for a low register instrument. The Eflat bass in those days was not considered to be a solo instrument and a performance even of such musicality, which the Slaithwaite lad invariably gave, was regarded by the audience as something of a novelty.

From time to time I was also approached to play solos in variety concerts mainly in church and chapel halls. One of the more memorable concerts was in a chapel hall on the outskirts of Barnsley. Along with the other performers I was expected to do my turn surrounded by a wooden frame about 3 feet square, suspended by long strings from the ceiling. The frame was supposed to represent a television screen, TV being in its infancy and quite a novelty then. The singers and some of the other performers had no problem in meeting this bizarre request. For me it was not so simple as I was expected to face obliquely through the frame with the trombone slide poking through. Several times I managed to catch the frame edge with the slide which set the whole contraption swinging wildly and in danger of collapse.

In those days brass bands played on so-called high pitch instruments with A at 452.5 Hertz, a hang-over from Victorian times. As with orchestras, pianos were tuned to concert pitch with A at 440 Hertz (referred to in the brass band world as low pitch). Therefore tuning a high pitch trombone to match a piano could be a chancy business. The difference between the two pitches is by no means negligible. The piano only had to be a shade flat to require the trombone tuning slide to be pulled out so far it was in danger of dropping out. Several times when doing my solo I could hear a soft buzzing sound behind my left ear due to a slight escape of air past the over-extended tuning slide. Mum and Dad unexpectedly solved this problem by buying me a brand new Boosey & Hawkes Imperial trombone in high pitch, but importantly, it came complete with an additional low pitch tuning slide. I knew absolutely nothing of their planned generous gesture. It was only when they returned from holiday in Southsea that they revealed they had stopped off at Boosey & Hawkes's shop in London's Regent Street and ordered it on the spot. I was absolutely dumbstruck, but so excited that I could hardly wait for its delivery at Clayton West railway station about a week later. This instrument retailed for £52-10s-0d (£52.50), a sizeable sum in those days. The new trombone had a larger bore than the old 'pea-shooters' that I'd played so far. Consequently, the tone was mellow and ringing but far less hard and strident than the old instruments. It was easy to blow and the slide action was light making this new trombone a joy to play.

The end of my full time membership of Clayton West Band was forced upon me soon after I started work at the local Park Mill Colliery. I was working underground and was also committed to attending Barnsley Technical College. My academic workload was a heavy one as I had determined that I ultimately wanted to study at university, and winning a scholarship was vital. One complete day on paid release from work together with 3 evenings per week was the demanding technical college schedule. In addition, there was always set homework to be completed, so attendance at regular band practices was out of the question. I did continue to play with the band on occasional engagements including the odd contest – even the National Finals in London some years later. News soon travelled round the brass band world that I was no longer full time at Clayton West and for quite a long period the house was besieged by band secretaries attempting to sign me. Laurence Mann, Skelmanthorpe's band secretary and a class bass trombonist (later with Carlton Main Frickley Colliery) was particularly persuasive. Of course, a full time commitment was out of the question, but having my own instrument allowed me to freelance with many bands including Skelmanthorpe, Emley, Flockton, Woolley Colliery, Hade Edge, Honley, Royston New Monkton Colliery and Carlton Main Frickley Colliery. At this time, my wardrobe at home contained a selection of uniforms lent by the various bands. On one occasion I had no fewer than 5 uniforms stowed away and not one of them was anywhere near a decent fit! At several contests I'll admit that I appeared illegally and signed the name of players registered with those bands. The original test pieces, which gave me the greatest thrill were Lorenzo, Coriolanus, Labour and Love, The Three Musketeers, along with the transcriptions of Lizst's Les Preludes, The Works of Mendelssohn and Berlioz's Les Franc Juges. These pieces I found exciting but very demanding, as I didn't have many rehearsals to prepare.

Playing as a guest with so many bands gave me an early rare insight into the mysterious world of conducting. For me, the most terrifying character was the old warhorse Noel Thorpe, who in 1938 had taken Slaithwaite Band to the very pinnacle of success with their win in the British Open Championship at Belle Vue. He had a ferocious temper if things weren't to his liking, and a withering look could reduce the stoutest of players to a shaking jelly. Amongst the other conductors I remember were Willie Kaye (no relation to my former violin teacher) and Harry Mileman at Skelmanthorpe, Charlie Westerby (formerly solo cornet with Brighouse & Rastrick) at Flockton, and Albert Robinson at Hade Edge. Albert was one of the old school of conductors who wore an out-of-fashion bandmasters black 'frock' coat with a high collar and dark red sash round the midriff. On the platform he always carried his cornet in his right hand. This allowed him to 'bump up' the solo cornets in a forte tutti passage. He had to turn the pages of the musical score with his left hand, consequently he didn't use a baton. He had lost his own front teeth, and in order for him to blow the cornet it was rumoured that he himself had fashioned a special false set from gutta-percha. Despite my work, study, and freelance banding commitments, I still found time for the occasional private lesson with Grenville at Brighouse and Rastrick. Eventually I had the opportunity to play engagements with that band when Bill Beverley (if memory serves me correctly), their second trombone was ill for a period.

Playing in brass bands wasn't always deadly serious and there were many amusing incidents. One I remember well, concerned Sid Orr an Eflat bass player with Clayton West band, which at the time had just received a new set of 4 basses from the Coal Industry Welfare Organisation. The first outing for the new instruments was a Saturday open-air concert in Normanton Park. That day Sid blew his heart out, but the instrument's response was feeble to say the least. This lack of 'oomph' worried Sid all weekend for he assumed that he had inadvertently damaged the instrument in some way. However, he confided in no-one. On the following Monday he mentioned to his wife that she had forgotten to provide the customary sandwiches. She replied that she had put them as usual down the large bell of the bass for easy transportation. An immediate search and shaking of the instrument revealed they had passed right around the first bend and lodged inside the instrument out of sight. No wonder the bass produced hardly a grunt! Needless to say, the retrieval of the now stale sandwiches made Sid a very relieved man indeed.

Writing of bass players reminds me of Sid's colleague Bflat bass player Wilf Addy. Wilf was built like a house, standing well over 6 feet tall and weighing in at approaching 20 stones – he made the massive Bflat bass look like a cornet in his hands. Wilf was a former euphoniumist and was an excellent player, capable of a feat which I'm sure only he could achieve. If he felt peckish during a performance he'd produce a pork pie from his pocket, take a great bite of it during a couple of bars rest, then continue playing. What the interior of his instrument must have been like doesn't bear thinking about!

An annual event which I always looked forward to with eager anticipation, was the Whit Friday pilgrimage made by many Yorkshire bands to the villages lying on the Lancashire side of the Pennines. 'Processions of Witness' by members of the many village chapels and churches had been held there for generations, Charlotte Bronte mentioning these in her novel Shirley. The processions were always headed by a band. In view of the early start, a breakfast in the schoolroom was usually provided. On one occasion I remember lettuce sandwiches - not very filling for a hungry young bandsman. Marching round the district could be a tiring affair particularly in an area noted for its steep hills. Stops were made at strategic points where several hymns would be rendered to band accompaniment. The morning's proceedings closed with lunch being provided in the schoolroom. During the afternoon the band played a series of selections interspersed with games and sports for the younger chapel members. A tea then rounded off the band's contracted commitment.

For me the highlight of the day was the band's participation in the March Contests, which were held in the open air begun in the early evening and continuing well into the hours of darkness. These were held in something like 20 venues and were 'all comers' events in which the lowliest junior band could compete on equal terms against the giants such as Black Dyke Mills, Brighouse & Rastrick, Besses, Fodens etc. With careful planning and a bit of luck to ensure the coach could make it relatively unhindered along the crowded roads it was possible to play at a dozen or so venues. Even in my day, without the use of mobile phones, planning the routes for maximum participation was a logistical triumph – more so now I gather. Beer and sandwiches on the coach were essential to maintain energy levels during the long evening. I know I've forgotten some of the venues I played but remember well those at Delph, Uppermill, Greenfield, Dobcross, Lees and Mossley. All the contests drew enormous enthusiastic crowds and for those interested in marches, it was a bonanza occasion. The popular choices were The Senator, Knight Templar, The Cossack, Mephistopheles, BB&CF, Roll Away Bet, Punchinello, Cornish Cavalier amongst many others. The atmosphere is hard to describe in detail, but would be best summed up as a massive mobile musical carnival. One was constantly bumping into friends and acquaintances from rival bands and catching up for a chat or the latest gossip. For me, these happy events remain imprinted on my mind and are some of the most enjoyable and exciting times I have enjoyed in music. Tiring, enormously satisfying, and requiring 3 days to recover!

Although I moved into orchestral playing some years later first with the trombone then later with the double bass, what I had learnt in brass bands laid the foundations for a long career in music, this most demanding of disciplines. But, more than that, my time in brass bands gave me tremendous enjoyment and great enthusiasm for music making. I count myself lucky to have stumbled, by chance, into this wonderful movement.

A Widening Musical Horizon

By the early 1950's I'd become very interested in dance music and jazz. BBC's Jazz Club was broadcast early on Saturday evening, a programme I eagerly anticipated. I was an avid reader of the long established Melody Maker and the upstart New Musical Express. Between them, these media streams fuelled my knowledge of this daring departure from musical orthodoxy.

Although modern jazz and bepop were being developed, British jazz bands were mainly playing so-called traditional jazz. The most popular bands were led by Humphrey Lyttleton, Joe Daniels, Freddie Randall, Sid Phillips and Mick Mulligan along with outfits such as the Yorkshire Jazz Band, the Crane River Jazz band and the Avon City Stompers. The ballroom dancing craze was still going strong and the big bands playing mainly swing numbers, broadcast regularly from the large dance halls such as the Hammersmith Palais and the Tower Ballroom, Blackpool. These excellent bands were led by the likes of Ted Heath, Joe Loss, Geraldo, Ken Mackintosh and Kenny Baker. I was absolutely astounded by the technical brilliance of dance band musicians. The range, dexterity and superb tone of trombonists like Don Lusher and George Chisholm left most brass band exponents standing. Of course the skills of those playing in local dance bands, which were usually much smaller outfits than the big bands were also excellent musicians.

Membership of my first dance band playing trombone, occurred whilst still at Penistone Grammar School. A school friend and accomplished dance band pianist, John Fisher was already leading a small group, but sadly the name now escapes me. Rehearsals were held at Dogley Lane chapel schoolroom in

Kirkburton, a village out in the country about 5 miles from Huddersfield. The band's existing line-up was 2 saxes, 2 trumpets and piano with another Penistonian John Halstead on drums. The only other member I recall was a chap called George Tricket on trumpet. With a thin chiselled face and greying hair he seemed positively ancient, but was probably only in his 40's. John invited me to join and at my first rehearsal I had the shock of my life to discover that the trombone parts in dance music were all written in the bass clef – a complete mystery to me. I felt such a fool that I was unable to sight read in this clef and I hardly blew a note during the 2 hour rehearsal. I took the parts away and worked at them furiously so that I was able to make a decent showing at my first engagement with the band a few days later – effectively I played my first job without rehearsal.

Despite our spruced up appearance in black DJ's, our standard of playing was not too accomplished by any stretch of the imagination but adequate enough for local 'hops'. Engagements started at 7.30pm with the early evening clientele drawn mainly from the younger end of the teenage group, who were not that critical of our performance. They were only too glad to be let out for the evening on their own, unsupervised. By the time the local pubs turned out we were well into our swing. After a few pints of John Smiths these newcomers, fortunately for us had lost their critical faculties. At 11.30pm, the time the *'Last Waltz'* came around, brass players generally had had enough – for a fact, my tired lip couldn't hit the top notes with any degree of certainty. Trombone parts in dance music seemed to be pitched at least a fourth higher than that generally found in the solo trombone part in brass bands, and it took me a while to become capable of handling this range without strain. The dances were mainly around the Huddersfield area and by the end of the dance, local bus services had ceased so I had the luxury of returning home by taxi.

One engagement I remember well was at Kirkheaton, on the outskirts of Huddersfield. The hall was a decent size, but the stage was far too narrow to accommodate the band in comfort. I was sitting at the front of the stage with the trumpets and saxes to my left and the piano and drums behind. The only way I could squeeze on was to have two beer crates supporting the outer legs of my chair. As the band members stamped their feet (dance band players without exception succumbed to this bad habit) the stage began swaying from side to side with the gap between the stage edge and the crates gradually widening. I felt in danger of falling through and at the end of each set I had to jump off the stage and reset the beer crates.

My next dance band, The Skyliners, was a far more professional affair. It was run by alto sax player Stuart Ferguson from Skelmanthorpe. Stuart was an excellent all-round musician and a superb trombonist, who I first met in the Skelmanthorpe Band. He had also played with the Woolley Colliery Band and for a short period with Morris Motors Band. The Skyliners could put on a big band performance with up to 16 or so players, but the numbers were variable depending upon the nature of the engagement. At busy times such as Christmas and the New Year, the band often split into two units with extra personnel being brought in to fill specific vacancies. The regular rhythm section was pianist Eddie Wray, drummer Ron Bowker, and bassist Gilbert Pell. Other popular band members were Peter Fretwell on trumpet, Stuart Gill on trombone and Arnold Wood on baritone sax.

One incident with this band is still vivid in my memory. We had been engaged to play a gig at Ryhill, a village out in the country between Barnsley and Wakefield. The band members were travelling in convoy in 2 taxis. Passing the grounds of Woolley Hall Training College in pitch darkness the second taxi broke down and its demise was not spotted by anyone in the leading car, which continued to the venue. I was in the leading car along with several other players, but none of the rhythm section. At the hall we took our time setting up awaiting the arrival of the second car. By the time the dance was scheduled to start there was no sign of the other band members, and it was obvious to us that something was amiss. The organiser was becoming concerned at our prevarication and eventually somewhat agitated. Finally, to appease him we made a start with a bizarre combination of instruments. Some half hour later the reinforcements arrived, having been picked up by our taxi retracing its route to base.

It was in this band that I took my first tentative steps as a double bass player. Knowing that I'd played the fiddle, Gilbert, taught me the basics of pizzicato bass in a few spare moments. Gilbert had quite an eye for the ladies and if he spotted a potential date, off he'd go to chat her up during a number where my trombone part wasn't that critical. The wiley guy realised I could then fill in for him on bass. Crucially, Gilbert's bass technique hadn't moved into the 20th century for he was still playing on an old 3 string bass tuned in fifths. Looking back, I guess that Gilbert had also been a fiddle player in his younger days and had simply adapted violin tuning to his bass. It was only later when I had the chance to play on a borrowed instrument that I suddenly discovered basses usually had 4 strings tuned in fourths. Sadly, all my earlier labours in terms of learning the instrument had been to no avail. I have often wondered in later years whether Gilbert's bass was by a famous maker and whether it would have been any good for orchestral work - in those days such niceties never occurred to me. In its favour, it was certainly at the latest, a 19th century instrument.

A new perspective opened up when I was awarded a West Riding County Major Scholarship to attended Leeds University. Although I was to study mining engineering, the trombone went with me when I left home for the first time. I was excited but also worried about my prospects in this new life, about which I knew absolutely nothing. I was a working class lad and wondered whether my contemporaries would be mainly public and fee paying independent school types. Naturally, I worried whether I would make friends and fit in. In the event, my fears were unfounded. Although I arrived straight off the coal face, fellow students on my course were generally from similar backgrounds, but most had entered direct from school. Music is a great leveller and the opportunity to meet up with others also having musical interests while studying a whole range of academic subjects, was certainly a bonus I didn't expect.

Freshers' Week was quite an eye-opener with the opportunity to join an eclectic range of mainstream and esoteric clubs and societies, which all had stalls set up in the Student's Union to entice the newcomer. I must confess that I played it pretty safe by first heading for the stall run by The Leeds University Union Music Society, known to all and sundry as The Music Soc. This catered for the serious end of the musical spectrum and embraced an orchestra, a large choral society, as well as smaller informal chamber groups. I also signed up with the Jazz Club having been attracted initially by the chance to sit in with some of the university's numerous jazz bands, as well as going off to various jazz concerts on outings organised by the club. What clinched it for me however, was the presence of 4 or 5 nice looking girls hanging around the stall! To present the appearance of a well-rounded student I also signed up with the The Mining Society, effectively my trade body, and to demonstrate my left of centre political leanings, The Labour Club. However, as music quickly came to dominate my university leisure time, political apathy soon set in.

It was with eager anticipation, but tempered with some trepidation, that I attended my first rehearsal with the orchestra. The personnel numbered something in the region of 50 players conducted by music lecturer, Frank

Mumby. Two trombonists from previous years were already in place. The principal trombone had an inflated opinion of his capabilities and adopted a rather superior attitude, but actually was a rather mediocre player. By contrast the second trombone was a girl, full of fun, a decent enough player, who had been a member of the Lancashire County Youth Orchestra. As we got to know each other I nicknamed her Masie after Masie Ringham, who was principal trombone with the Halle for many years. I think Masie was rather pleased to have me alongside, having suffered the principal trombone's condescending attitude during all of the past season's concerts. I settled myself in the bass trombone's chair and I enjoyed myself immensely tackling the bass trombone parts on a Bflat instrument – no Bflat/F combination instruments in those days. I remember the first piece I played as an orchestral trombonist was a super arrangement for full orchestra of Mozart's jolly overture Lucio Silla. At the end of the first term the concert in the University Great Hall was very well attended and received. The only other piece I can recall was Borodin's In the Steppes of Central Asia.

At the end of the first rehearsal of the second term Frank collared me to ask if I would be up to playing the trombone part in Poulenc's Trio for Trumpet, Horn and Trombone in the next concert. He explained that he had already offered the opportunity to my two senior colleagues, who had both declined on the grounds that it was too difficult. Although I'd never heard the piece before, I had a quick look at the part and agreed on the spot. Looking back, that was a bold, quite possibly foolish decision, as a quick glance at the printed part doesn't always reveal the potential dangers and hidden traps. My partners were to be fellow orchestra members, principal trumpet, Dennis Hill and principal horn Kerr Borthwick. Dennis, reading French, had been brought up in the Salvation Army band tradition and possessed a beautiful bell-like tone. Kerr was much older and was Senior Lecturer in Classics. He was a very accomplished player with an impish nature who could be found leading the Rag Day procession around Leeds city centre playing Onward Christian Soldiers or some such rousing piece. I practiced hard at the Poulenc for at least 30 minutes every day and as a small group we met up several times for a rehearsal with Frank. By the time the concert arrived we were feeling pretty confident that we could give a reasonable performance, barring serious accident.

The form of the concert was reminiscent of those popular in the 19th century, being a mixture of large choral works with two choruses from Hayden's Creation and A Festival Te Deum by Holst, as well as the orchestral items. Additionally, there were a variety of individual pieces including Schubert's Shepherd on the Rock. Following the interval, our trio was wedged between a Sonatina for Piano by Kenneth Leighton and Casella's Pupazzetti for Piano Duet. The hall was absolutely packed since friends of those singing in the large chorus also turned up in addition to the usual orchestra followers. Truth to tell, it was rather a nerve-racking occasion. When our turn came, the three of us with our brass instruments sat at the front of the stage, backed by the orchestra. The massed ranks of the chorus were behind us, and the sea of faces of the audience in front of us. I've a good idea how exposed concerto performers must feel! Rapturous and prolonged applause greeted the end of our performance with calls for an encore. The three of us smiled somewhat sheepishly, knowing that we hadn't prepared even a short piece for that unexpected eventuality. The respected and often feared music critic Ernest Bradbury of the Yorkshire Post, was quite complimentary when reviewing the concert in next day's edition of the newspaper, he wrote, *'three members of the orchestra Dennis Hill (trumpet), Kerr Borthwick (horn) and Edward Hellewell (trombone) played more than competently Poulenc's trio for those instruments'*. I'm not quite sure what he was expecting, for earlier in the review he wrote, *'indicative of a modern preference in instruments, the orchestra's woodwind and brass, which included three trombones, was of remarkably good quality'.*

During the period we were rehearsing the Poulenc I got to know Frank Mumby quite well. Although I cannot recall it now, I must have mentioned in passing that besides playing the trombone and previously the violin, I also had a nodding acquaintance with the double bass. Frank clearly had a good memory and at the start of next university concert season he asked me if I would be prepared to play the bass rather than the trombone. He had discovered that the previous bass player had graduated and there was in any case a surfeit of trombones. I attempted to wriggle out explaining that my bass playing had been confined to dance band pizzicato only and I'd never put a bow across the strings. *"Don't worry too much about that, you'll soon pick it up – and by the way, the society's bass and bow are in the practice room off Woodhouse Lane!"* was Frank's response. If only he had known of my complete incompetence on the instrument perhaps he would not have been so encouraging! So began my temporary excursion into the orchestra's lower strings.

I was entirely taken aback when I met up with the society's bass for the first time. There it was, leaning up in the corner of the practice room, and to me it appeared massive compared with the size I remembered Gilbert's bass being. Furthermore, I was absolutely horror struck to find the instrument had 4 strings. Closer inspection revealed strings reminiscent of ship's hawsers – actually, these were typical for the time. The two lower strings were large diameter wire wound gut and the upper two somewhat thinner, but still with quite large diameter gut. My heart sank further when I suddenly realised I didn't even know what notes the strings should be tuned to! I immediately shot off to the music section of the university's Brotherton Library and found the bass description in Grove's Dictionary of Music and Musicians to be a goldmine of information. I returned and tuned the bass using the practice room piano for pitch and then attempted to produce a sound with the bow. What a disappointment! Instead of the expected deep sonorous note, all I managed was a dreadful scratching noise. I realised immediately that the bow required considerable weight on the string, compared to what I remembered of the violin, and also that a spot of rosin on the bow might help it to grip. I shot off to Balmforth's string instrument shop near the centre of Leeds and picked up a block of Eugene Cruft's bass rosin. At the same time, for 2s 6d (12.5p), I bought How to Play the Double Bass, an extremely elementary 32 page tutor by Lew Stern in The First Step series. Such was the optimism of youth that I reckoned these two acquisitions would, in no time at all, guarantee my virtuosity on the bass. The next two weeks were to prove otherwise. Progress to say the least, was downright disappointing, particularly my inability to tackle the quicker passages. I felt that I ought to warn Frank of the situation, hoping that he would give me a reprieve. Quite the contrary, *"Oh don't worry too much about it, simplify the part as much as you need, just like the old bass players used to do"* was his advice. Clearly, he preferred a duff bass player to no bass player.

By the time the concert arrived, my printed copy of the bass part of Beethoven's Egmont Overture had the appearance of a code breaker's nightmare. I had added my extensive pencil crossings-out, alterations, scribbles, underlines, and arrows, together with the vital tiny numbers over the few remaining notes to indicate which finger I should use. The overture is not difficult for a reasonably competent performer, but for an absolute beginner it was a nightmare. The slow opening and first none-too quick allegro both have 4 flats on the stave, and my copy of How to Play the Double Bass let me down badly by only progressing as far as the E flat major (3 flats) scale. Consequently, I had to invent my own fingering system to attempt the part. The final allegro con brio section, although in the easy key of F major (1 flat) was really too quick for me to cope without extensive editing of the part. I reckon Beethoven would have had a fit if he'd seen what I had done to his composition. I can't remember what other pieces I had to face in my first bass concert, but I enjoyed immensely the feeling of providing the low notes of the orchestral sound, despite my dreadful technique and often suspect intonation. The remaining concerts I played with the orchestra were all on the bass and gradually, with practice and familiarity, my technique improved to what might best be described as mediocre.

Improvisation has never been my forte and the times I sat in on trombone with some of the university's traditional jazz bands were never very satisfying for me, and I'm sure even less so for the regular band members. I always felt much happier with a printed part, so I resorted to purchasing a book, 14 Dixieland Instrumentals for Trombone, including such favourites as Copenhagen, Ory's Creole Trombone and Tin Roof Blues also a copy of Glen Millers' 125 Jazz Breaks for Trombone both published by Herman Darewski. My idea was to memorize these tunes in order to give me at least a base to work from. Despite that, the outcome was disappointing. I noticed that most of the jazz players were of the 'rough and ready' type, mostly self-taught I would guess.

My urge to play jazz trombone was fulfilled when I was approached by Hedley Teale to join his band. Hedley was a superb clarinettist, who I had met in the university orchestra. I first really noticed him when he gave a superb performance of the clarinet obligato in Schubert's Shepherd on the Rock, which I mentioned earlier. The line up of his band was virtually standard New Orleans with a front line of trumpet, trombone and clarinet, backed by piano, bass, drums and banjo. Band parts for most of the jazz standards were available from a wide range of music publishers. The players, who were all trained and good music readers used these as a foundation. In addition to the gigs we played in the Leeds area, Hedley arranged many dates around Bradford, his home city. During my time at university I also enjoyed playing trombone on occasional weekends home with a traditional jazz band formed by my old mates in my home village. For many years, members of this band met for an annual re-union weekend – to the relief of our wives and partners, without instruments. This event illustrates nicely the lasting friendships that music can bring.

The Letter

Dear Edward,
I've always admired your playing. A vacancy has occurred in the trombone section of the Huddersfield Philharmonic Orchestra and the management committee has asked me to approach you with a view to you joining us.

So began the letter which came totally out of the blue from Joe Broadbent, who was principal trombone and also deputy conductor of the Huddersfield Philharmonic Orchestra. Those opening words I remember well, but after several house moves, the letter is now missing. At the time, naturally I was flattered. But hold on a minute, I couldn't have been that good or were they really that desperate? If the latter, he was kind enough never to let on!

The letter arrived shortly after I'd left university and I was back working in the coal mining industry as a management trainee, often on shift work. Musically, I wasn't doing much other than again playing regularly with the Skyliners dance band together with the occasional freelance job with brass bands. My only recent foray into the orchestral world had been the limited one at university. Student orchestras might have improved since then, but in those days they were without tradition and, by the very nature of their transient membership, could be rather scratch affairs. In contrast, the Huddersfield orchestra, founded in 1862 by the Rev. J.H. Thomas, and known then as Mr. Thomas's Band, had a fine musical tradition and it was a pretty competent outfit led by the redoubtable Madame Margaret Binns. Historically, the orchestra underwent a further name change to the Fitzwilliam Street Philharmonic Society before settling on its present name in 1885. Strictly speaking it is the orchestra of the Huddersfield Philharmonic Society and has a claim to be the UK's oldest non-professional orchestra.

Joe Broadbent was very active in the Huddersfield area's musical world, having originally been brought up in the brass band tradition. In his younger days he had led the locally famed 4H's trombone quartet, made up of the principal players from the four Holme Valley bands. The quartet's name was derived from the initial letter H of the four bands in question, Hade Edge, Honley, Holme and Hinchliffe Mill. I first came across Joe some years earlier at the Holmbridge quartet contest where he was a leading light on the organising committee. Even though he was no longer playing in brass bands, his bald head could usually be spotted at band contests and concerts.

In response to his letter, my meeting with him at his house in Honley one Sunday morning was for me, not only informative but encouraging. After welcoming me, his down to earth Yorkshire hospitality was immediate. *"I know you'll like a pot of tea and how about a nice drop of whisky in it to warm you up after your motorbike journey?"* were his warm welcoming words, and he then proceeded to cut me a massive slice of parkin. I took to Joe immediately, although I'm still not sure whether our meeting was to confirm that I would be suitable for the ***'job'*** or for him to *'sell'* me the orchestra. We had a long chat about my trombone playing career, during which he did reveal that he'd heard me performing solos on several occasions.

He talked at some length about the orchestra and its long history, and he made sure I realised it was somewhat ahead of its time, certainly for an amateur orchestra in the late 1950's, having just completed a tour to the Brunswick area of Germany. The orchestra he related, was also proud of the fact that along with an augmented Huddersfield Vocal Union, they had not long ago given Huddersfield's first performance of Beethoven's Choral Symphony. To this day, given Huddersfield's outstanding musical tradition (think first of Huddersfield Choral Society's world wide reputation), I find it incredible that this work was not performed in the town until the 1950's. Joe assured me that my lack of orchestral experience, in particular my inability to read the alto clef, wouldn't necessarily be a handicap. He reminded me that the orchestra's bass trombonist was an excellent player, Stuart Noble from Cumberworth, something I had known already but had forgotten. I was acquainted with Stuart from earlier years when he too was in the brass band world. I had also met him when I was working at Park Mill colliery before going to university. Stuart was employed there as a colliery electrician. *"I can see you settling in nicely between Stuart and myself,"* was Joe's reassuring remark. With such an obvious invitation I simply hadn't the heart to refuse, even if I had wanted to. On my way out and almost as an afterthought Joe said, *"Oh, just one thing, the orchestra's conductor is a fiery Welshman called Billy Rees – he's prone to pick on individuals, but just show him you can play and you'll have no trouble with him."* At that point I began to wonder what I'd let myself in for!

My initial contact with William Rees the professional conductor, known to orchestra members as Billy, was as nerve-wracking as I had imagined. Rehearsals then were held in a large second storey room in Railway Street, right in the town centre leading into St. George's Square which is fronted by the magnificent façade of the town's railway station. On arrival at my first rehearsal, Joe introduced me to Billy whose opening gambit was, *"So you're the young man Joe's been telling me about."* He followed this immediately with, to my way of thinking, a remark of some menace, *"Well, we'll see what you're made of with the overture."* Although I'd never played Wagner's Flying Dutchman overture, I'd heard it several times and so it was not entirely unfamiliar. The piece opens with a short burst of 'scrubbing' high up in the violins quickly followed by the horns proclaiming the first major theme. Some 7 bars later was my chance to impress. Along with my trombone mates and the tuba I blasted out the same theme as loudly as I could without *'overblowing'*. This wall of sound appeared to take Billy by surprise, but at the completion of the trombones' effort he looked straight across at me, smiled and gave the thumbs up sign. After that I never had a moment's trouble from Billy.

Billy's bark was in fact far worse than his bite, and despite his very occasional sharp words if things weren't to his liking, the players simply loved him. He had a marvellous relaxed manner and certainly could extract the very best from his charges. He knew the orchestra and the orchestral world inside out. Originally a violinist he had played with the BBC, the Royal Liverpool Philharmonic and principally the Halle orchestra during Sir Hamilton Harty's conductorship between the wars. Under Harty's direction the Halle was re-established as one of Europe's leading orchestras. Billy was greatly influenced by Harty and he went on to take a Masters Course in conducting at the Royal Manchester College of Music under Felix Weingartner. His subsequent conducting of the Municipal Concerts in Manchester brought collaboration with many famous artists including Kreisler, Heifetz,

Rachmaninoff, Menhuin and many others. His conducting skills were not solely limited to the orchestra, for he also served as conductor of the Manchester Philharmonic Choir and of the Manchester Beecham Operatic Chorus.

At opportune moments during rehearsal Billy loved to tell anecdotes and these delightful stories enlivened what otherwise, could have been a dull moment. On one occasion he recalled with pride how Weingartner had paid him a compliment during a master class by referring to him as a natural Brahms conductor. He then went on to relate how he had paid Arthur Catterall a fee of 30 guineas out of his own pocket to play Brahms Violin Concerto, not so much as to allow the audience the pleasure of hearing it but to give himself the opportunity to conduct it. Arthur Catterall is hardly remembered now, but many believe he was probably the finest English born violinist of the late 19th and early 20th centuries, having been leader of the legendary Queen's Hall Orchestra under Sir Henry Wood, the Halle and the BBC Symphony Orchestra. In addition to his illustrious orchestral involvement he pursued a distinguished solo career beginning as a child prodigy at the age of 8, when he performed the Mendelssohn concerto in Manchester!

One of my favourite musical stories concerns Harty, and even today I have a quiet chuckle whenever I think of Billy recounting it. The Halle was accompanying one of the world's most respected and admired concert pianists Artur Schnabel, who like Catterall, also made his public debut at the age of 8. During a performance of the Brahms B flat concerto he had a lapse of memory and in the final section missed out two bars completely. Harty had such rapport with the orchestra that he was able to cover up the mistake. Afterwards Schnabel confided in Harty that the Halle was almost as good as the Berlin Philharmonic. Quick as a flash Harty replied, *"no we are better, we usually play two more bars of the concerto."*

At the start of every rehearsal when the players were comfortably seated (players in those days didn't dare turn up late for a rehearsal!) Billy usually welcomed everyone with some light-hearted comments. He always referred to the trombone section as *'The Navy'*, apparently as Harty had done some 50 years earlier. For some reason or other I had asked permission to miss one rehearsal, which was granted. The following week he opened proceedings with a smile towards me and the jocular comment, *"ladies and gentlemen of the orchestra, you'll be delighted to observe that this week we have The Navy back with us at full strength."*

I'd been playing with the orchestra for a couple of years or so and a public reference to 'The Navy' occurred as a result of a memorable incident during a performance in Huddersfield Town Hall on 9th April 1960 of The Royal Hunt and Storm from Berlioz's opera, The Trojans. The strings completely lost themselves and minor chaos began to develop, which could easily have led to a complete breakdown. Billy seized the initiative and quick as a flash pointed to the trombones and mouthed the word *"Now"*. We knew immediately what our response should be, which resulted in one of the loudest unison entries imaginable. At this signal the strings recovered their place and the orchestra immediately pulled itself together. After the applause had died down Billy brought the trombone section to its feet, turned to the audience and proclaimed in a voice which could be heard in the far Upper Gallery, *"thank God for The Navy."*

On another later occasion after I had moved into the bass section, my former colleagues in the trombone section misjudged the time and failed to return to the stage after the concert's interval. As was customary, this little group had shot off for a 'swift half' in The County pub opposite Huddersfield Town Hall where the concert was being held. Billy had returned to the podium and, realising that these forces were missing, held up proceedings. Eventually three shame-faced, flustered offenders slunk onto the stage. Billy turned to the audience and announced, *"Ladies and Gentlemen, you need not have worried - I knew The Navy would not let us down!"*

During my time in the trombone section and Billy's tenure, the orchestra performed several fairly rare works including Wagner's The Holy Supper of the Apostles, in collaboration with the renowned Colne Valley Male Voice Choir. A concert featured The Fenton Ladies Choir singing Folk Songs of the Four Seasons by Vaughan Williams and Thomas Pitfield's A Sketchbook of Women. Amongst the orchestral rarities were A Faust Overture by Wagner, Eric Fenby's Rossini on Ilkla Moor, the first performance of Romantic Overture by Willi Woller and Saint-Saens's Overture La Princesse Jaune. Billy was a champion of Berlioz and included such works as the overtures Waverley, le Corsaire, and The Royal Hunt and Storm.

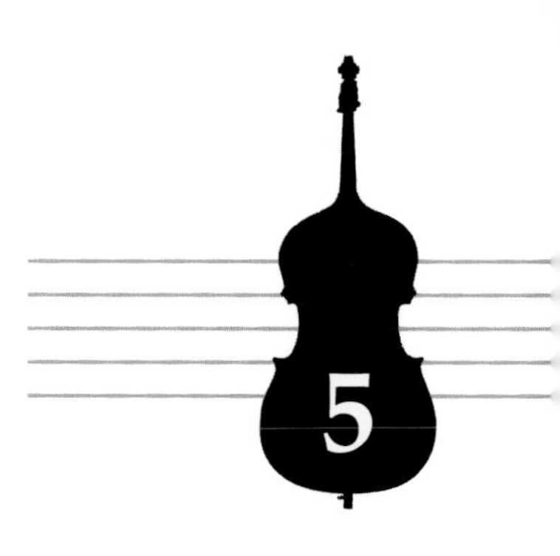

Tha Can't Get Much Lower Than This

Orchestral trombonists don't usually suffer from overwork! The first composer to employ the instrument in a symphony was Beethoven in his ground breaking fifth. Incidentally, he went on to even greater things with his bass trombone solo in the Choral (ninth) symphony. Vast libraries of music composed prior to this time other than the odd opera or the occasional church piece, are effectively barren for the trombone. With my background in the brass band and dance band worlds where one is kept pretty busy, I began to discover that long periods of inactivity inherent in orchestral playing really didn't suit my temperament.

Since leaving university where I'd had a brief spell on the double bass, my interest in this instrument had continued. I'd managed to borrow a bass (actually it was on a life-time loan if I needed it) from the Hallas family, garage owners in Grange Moor a village on the outskirts Huddersfield. During the three years that I was playing trombone in 'The Phil' I continued to practice the bass, although none too seriously. Nevertheless, despite a pretty awful technique, I achieved a passable level of proficiency, entirely self-taught. At breaks in rehearsal I used to wander over and chat to the players in the bass section. It was during one of these interludes that sub-principal bass Harold Bray, a gas fitter by trade, pointed a gnarled finger to a minim on the ledger line below the bass clef and pronounced in a thick Yorkshire accent, *"tha can't get much lower than this,"* a memorable sentence indeed, and one which for ever has remained with me.

Not often does an individual marry the first person with whom they have a romantic liaison. Choosing an instrument for life is much the same. I had a relationship with 3 instruments, the violin, the trombone and the clarinet, although the latter was more of a wild fling, before I knew the bass and me were together for life. I was really getting bored in the trombone section and I was in truth, looking for a way out. It was shortly after Harold had made his memorable remark that I casually mentioned that I was teaching myself the bass and that I wouldn't mind joining the section if they'd have me. Section principal Bamford Hoyle sprang into action immediately, and thrust his Italian Ceruti masterpiece in my direction and encouraged me to show them what I could do. Two or three major scales and a few bars of The Elephant and I was in! Of course the Orchestra Secretary George Platt was keen to point out that I'd have to wait until the start of next season since a replacement would have to be found for me in the trombone section. This suited me fine since it allowed me the time to concentrate on a spot of serious bass practice.

During the summer months when The Phil had its break, I travelled more or less on a weekly basis over to Bamford's house in Marsden at the head of the Colne Valley. Occasionally as a change to routine, Bamford and his wife Lilian came over to us at Emley. I'll be forever grateful to Bamford for taking me under his wing and putting me on the straight and narrow on some of the intricacies of the bass. We didn't do much in the way of scales, arpeggios and studies, which with the benefit of hindsight was a serious omission. Instead, he had me concentrating on learning bass technique through excerpts from the orchestral repertoire. For this purpose he gave me a battered copy of A Scrap Book for the use of Students of the Double Bass by John Reynolds. This is undated, but an indication of its age can be gauged from an advertisement on the back cover for a new Hawkes Panormo Bass described as used in the Private Band of Her late Majesty the Queen [Victoria] costing £25 4s 0d for a 4 stringer and £23 2s 0d for a 3 string version.

Bamford was a true bass enthusiast and this trait no doubt rubbed off on me. He was extremely knowledgeable on basses and their makers, and he would chase off all over the place if he obtained a sniff of an old one which might be a potential purchase. However, as a true Yorkshireman the price had to be right! He made several decent finds. His luckiest was a bass he tracked down to a school at Swinton in South Yorkshire in the early 1970's during the time he was a peripatetic bass teacher for the West Riding. The instrument, with a broken neck, had been thrown into a storeroom and was in a severely distressed state. He repaired all the cracks himself and restored it pretty well other than fixing the neck. He got a repairer from Leeds to take that on, resulting in a neck graft. Whether he realised it at the time he purchased it I'm not sure, but subsequently it was authenticated by Jack Pamplin of Thwaites the bass specialists, as a genuine Italian, the maker I've now forgotten. Without doubt, Bamford realised a handsome profit when he sold it on commission through Thwaites. Within a few weeks the bass had found a new home in America.

In addition to his Italian Ceruti of which he was extremely proud, he also owned an English Cole, both of these being featured in Raymond Elgar's book Looking at the Double Bass [pp. 62&63 and 161&162]. At the time I moved into the bass section of The Phil I was still playing on the borrowed instrument and I was eager to purchase the Cole, which he had been thinking of selling. Bamford refused me simply because it had an elusive 'buzz' on certain notes. Despite his patient detective work he was unable to trace the source and he felt he could not let his protégé have what might in the future, be a defective instrument. With the benefit of hindsight I really ought to have insisted he put his misgivings to one side and sell it to me. The bass he eventually sold to Peter Leah, principal bass of the BBC Northern Orchestra, now re-named the BBC Philharmonic Orchestra.

Although Bamford was old enough to be my father, as time went by a friendship of true equals developed. However, I was also acutely aware how difficult he could be at times and sometimes rather stubborn. If he took a dislike to someone there was no earthly way that person could ever rehabilitate themselves in Bamford's world. I remember an incident when he was making a free distribution of his home brewed rosin amongst members of the section. He deliberately and pointedly omitted one person who he thought of as a big-headed upstart and who he had simply no time for. Afterwards he turned to me and said in a quiet voice, *"that bugger's never going to get owt from me."*

Billy Rees's connection with Huddersfield Philharmonic dated back to the dark days of the Second World War, when in 1943 he stepped in at short notice to conduct the orchestra in a concert of Beethoven's Symphony No 5, Greig's Piano Concerto and the then, very popular 'Warsaw' Concerto by Richard Addinsell. However, his appointment as permanent professional conductor occurred at the end of hostilities when he took the podium for the orchestra's Winter concert on 30th March 1946. For me and I'm sure for all members, the 18th April 1964 was a sad day, for this was when we bade farewell to Billy in his final concert. The few short speeches and presentation to close the proceedings ensured there were quite a few lumps in throats and a profusion of tears. Billy was a true professional, who approached his task with a confidence born of a long apprenticeship in a myriad of music making activities. Yet despite his undoubted musical stature, his approach to music was always unassuming and he gave the impression that he was so lucky to be outstanding at something he genuinely enjoyed. It was this infectious enthusiasm which spilled over into his players' performances and I can't ever recall an occasion when the players grumbled about him – knowing orchestral players, that's some tribute. On a personal level, Billy was an inspiration. His rehearsals were a pleasure to attend and no matter what the circumstance, Billy could always find an amusing story to illustrate the point. He certainly left a legacy of a happy and extremely competent group of players.

The new conductor was Arthur Butterworth, a composer and superbly able musician, who I suspect knew he had a difficult act to follow. He didn't have the flamboyant approach Billy thrived on, but he tackled the new challenge with a calmness backed by considerable musical authority and knowledge. In complete contrast to Billy, he very rarely mentioned his musical background. However, it was during one of his early rehearsals that he mentioned to the trumpets that he wanted a fanfare similar in style to the one written for the cornets and occurring towards the end of a fairly obscure brass band march The Captain by Eugene Verner. I realised that such an intimate knowledge of this piece could only have been gained by a person who had been at the sharp end of the brass band world – probably I guessed, as a cornet player. I learned later that my supposition had been entirely correct.

The programme chosen for his first concert on 7th November 1964 was a solid, no-nonsense mainstream affair, but unusually included two symphonies. The first half of the concert opened with Wagner's overture Rienzi and continued with Haydn's Symphony No. 99 in E flat and Richard Strauss's Horn Concerto No.1. The Adagio for Strings by Samuel Barber and a lesser known work of Tchaikovsky, his Symphony No.2 in C minor [The Little Russian] formed the second half. Concert programmes in succeeding years were still dominated by the popular classical and romantic composers. An occasional foray was made into unfamiliar territory and I therefore became acquainted, but not over enamoured, with some works of Glazounov, Malcolm Arnold, Prokofiev, Jarnefeldt and Dohnanyi. I guess that Arthur had a hand in guiding the committee in a more adventurous direction.

Within a very short time of Arthur's arrival he showed a touching (possibly misplaced) faith in my bass playing ability. As conductor of several choral societies in the Bradford, Leeds and Halifax areas, he was responsible for fixing the small accompanying orchestras. It was through his invitation to join this select band that I experienced my first freelance bass engagements. The first concert I played in this capacity was for a performance of Mendelssohn's Elijah at a large chapel on the outskirts of Bradford. The format of all these choral events was the same. An afternoon rehearsal with the choir was always followed by a couple of hours break for tea, usually a decent spread provided by the lady committee members. The performance in front of a usual capacity audience, who had paid anything from 2s 6d to 7s 6d for a ticket and a programme for 6d, occupied the evening.

It was during some of these tea breaks that I chatted to Arthur and learned a little of his background. As a boy he began his successful musical career with several undistinguished brass bands in the Manchester district. The trombone was his first instrument, despite his arms being too short to push the slide out to reach the 7th position. During one of these tea breaks, he clearly enjoyed telling me the story of his trombone misfortune on a Whit Friday march at one of the Pennine chapels. After struggling up and down steep hills on the march, the instrument simply became too much of a burden for his youthful frame and quite literally he caught the end of the slide in the points of the tramlines. The slide buckled and was of no further use without drastic surgery. Whilst the instrument was away being repaired he was given a cornet with which he became fascinated, consequently he never returned to the trombone. He was clearly a talented young player and musically knowledgeable for in 1939 at the age of 16 he won the Alex Owen Scholarship, which gave him cornet lessons and the opportunity to study composition. At about this time he joined the famous Besses O' Th' Barn band where his playing career resumed for a short period after war service, which was then followed by study at the Royal Manchester College of Music. His professional career continued as a trumpeter in the Scottish National and the Halle Orchestras.

As a conductor Arthur had stage presence without being ultra demonstrative. He didn't go in for exaggerated movements yet he could communicate to the orchestra the performance subtleties he was looking for. For me, two particular attributes set him apart from many conductors I've experienced. The first, having decided what tempo he considered most appropriate for a particular passage and having set that in rehearsal, one could rely absolutely on that tempo being the one he would set in the performance. In contrast, some conductors tend to speed up for the performance, no doubt due to an adrenalin rush. This can be quite unsettling for players, many of whom have their own built-in metronomes. A different tempo from that practiced in rehearsals can lead to very scrappy execution especially in fast, tricky and unison passages. Secondly, he always gave a clear downbeat for the first beat of the bar, no doubt influenced by the time he served in the brass band world. I, along with many orchestral players I've spoken to, look for that from the conductor if nothing else! Taking his musical knowledge and competence for granted, looking back to a time 50 years ago, my over-riding memory of Arthur is one of a man who was totally in control on the podium, a man who inspired confidence in his players, but at the same time was completely unassuming. For me a true gentleman!

I still have in my possession a letter dated 17th May 1965, which Arthur Butterworth wrote to me after I had had to cancel a date to play Haydn's Creation for him which coincided with the time when my second son, Julian, made his appearance into the world:

> Dear Mr Hellewell,
>
> I must congratulate you and your wife on the birth of your big boy! [Julian weighed in at 10lb 9oz] I hope all now runs smoothly for you at home.
> If he is so big I think he most certainly will be a Bass-player (they do say bass-playing runs in families you know) – although if he really wants to make a name for himself in music there are even more opportunities for BASSOON players - and they need big hands too!
> However, here is a small token to begin his instrument fund with (he'll certainly need to start saving soon if he is to play a big instrument).
>
> Yours sincerely,
> Arthur Butterworth

I think the letter says it all about the man – simply a super guy. Incidentally, enclosed was a ten shilling note, a fair sized sum then. Sadly, Julian became neither a bassist nor bassoonist!

Since writing the above, I was saddened to learn of Arthur Butterworth's death in November 2014. The obituary recorded that he ceased his connection with the Huddersfield Philharmonic Orchestra in 1993, but continued with many musical activities including returning to his roots by conducting the National Youth Brass Band. He lived to the ripe old age of 91, and posterity will best remember him as a prolific romantic composer, his works including 7 symphonies. Sadly, today romantic works by modern composers hardly get a look in – enough said!!

6

The Orchestral Machine

> These are to give notice that at Mr John Bannister's House (now called the musick school) over against the George Tavern in Whyte Fryres, this present Monday, will be performed music by excellent masters, beginning at precisely four of the clock in the afternoon.

The above advertisement in the London Gazette on the 30th December 1672 announced, what is now regarded as the earliest public concert. Since that time literally millions of public concerts ranging from the dire to the sublime, must have taken place – many of those that we now come to know by the title Symphony Concert or Orchestral Concert.

A modern symphony orchestra of some 80 players seated under the bright stage lights of a concert hall is without doubt, an impressive sight. Rank upon rank of antique and modern string instruments - violin, viola, cello and double bass shimmering in a variety of hues from black, through dark brown, light brown, orange to red. Behind them the diverse woodwind family - silver flutes, black oboes and clarinets and reddish-brown bassoons all showing off impressive complex silver keywork. Bringing up the rear left flank the brass section sit in elevated splendour with their shiny, burnished trumpets, trombones and tuba. The rear centre position is taken by the percussion section, the artillery of the orchestra. The percussionists stand by ready to do battle with a bewildering arsenal of equipment - huge shiny copper timpani, big bass drum, side drum, cymbals, gong and a host of lesser weaponry. The rear right flank is occupied by the four or sometimes five horns, their intricate coiled pipes glistening, some a deep copper colour, others a pale golden yellow. The magnificent sound washes over the audience. Yes, these impressive forces provide the concertgoer hopefully with a memorable experience, not just aurally but visually as well.

Despite operating in the cultural and artistic field the orchestra is nevertheless akin to a complex piece of machinery. In such a machine, the component parts must each operate at optimum efficiency and combine in a pre-arranged sequence. Any failure or mal-function of one part of a machine may result in undesirable consequences, even a total breakdown. So it is with an orchestra. Each individual has an assigned part to play and any failure to render that part accurately, although not necessarily fatal to a performance, will certainly detract from a perfect rendition.

The concertgoer could be forgiven for thinking that the beautiful sounds emanating from this dynamic body, result from each and every player contributing willingly to the common cause in an atmosphere of peace and satisfaction. Well, I'll let you into a secret. Beneath this apparent tranquillity sometimes lie disagreements, discord and discontent. Why do we have to play this bloody piece, it's total crap; Why did we have to turn up for a 5pm rehearsal before the scheduled 7.30pm kick off, I'm buggered now; Why does he (the conductor) take it at snail's pace, time for a nap I reckon. These and similar grouses are the small grievances which players often direct at the organisers and conductors, but are generally wise enough to keep amongst themselves.

However, these murmurings may not be the only discontent within the orchestra. Sometimes there is underlying tension between players and disagreements are often on sectional lines. The players in the various sections often behave like tribesmen with a fierce loyalty to their own kind and light-hearted banter is not uncommon. On rare occasions, disagreements become rather more serious and members of one tribe will gang up on another and disparage the musical efforts of their rivals.

It is only when one has played with the same orchestra for a while that one gets a sense of the undercurrent – who likes who, who dislikes who, who fancies who, who has left who, who is trying to get into bed with who, who are the 'pratts', who are the 'characters'. It's in the orchestra that you see a mirror image of life outside, but in very sharp relief.

I've often thought about the reasons why players have chosen a particular instrument. Generalisations can be misleading, but I believe that a person's character, genes if you like, has a significant influence. The brass section for instance, provides the dramatic effect often at double forte and in a declamatory style. For this job a shrinking violet wouldn't be much use. No, it's a confident, extrovert character that's likely to succeed in that role. On the other hand a shy diffident person is more likely to find security and anonymity amongst the back desks of the 2nd violins. Careful observation over many years allows me to make some comment on the character of the various sections, and on the manner in which they go about their work.

Numerically, the strings make up the bulk of the orchestra and comprise violin, viola, cello and bass sections with the violins being subdivided into firsts and seconds. By their nature strings can play for extended periods, and it is their job to 'carry the tune'. In contrast the brass for instance, whose stamina is rather more limited by the instrument's physical demands, are best able to contribute mainly in shorter bursts, and are therefore used principally for dramatic effect or when additional volume is called for.

String players with the exception of the bass section, are occasionally looked on by many as a pansy bunch. In my experience, first violinists can exude an aura of superiority, simply because they play the top line which is usually the recognisable melody – the one the audience hum afterwards. They are undoubtedly extremely competitive creatures and whatever their station in the desk rankings they often believe they should be in a higher position, if not the orchestra leader. They can fight like ferrets in a bag to gain the advantage over a potential rival. It's not unknown for downright underhand tricks to have been employed in that quest. I've known an instance of one individual during the break between rehearsal and performance, rubbing out the pencil bowings on a rival's part and substituting 'duff' bowings. In another case I've been told of a couple of pages of music disappearing during the break, much to the chagrin of the player suddenly discovering this during the concert.

Second fiddlers on the other hand can suffer from an inferiority complex mainly due to the attitude of the firsts. The second violin section is the ideal spot for those of a nervous disposition to hide away, safe in the knowledge that they are towards the back of the stage and any hesitancy on their part won't be spotted by the audience. Having said that there are however, usually some very competent performers in the section.

The viola section contains the slave labourers of the orchestra, for these oppressed individuals hardly get a bar's rest. They are always on the go, playing in the upper register to help out the second fiddles, the next minute down in the lower register assisting the cellos. If they were paid on a per note basis they'd be the orchestra's equivalent of merchant bankers. Viola players, or to refer to them by their posh name, violists, are considered by some to be failed violinists. Don't believe that one, there's some extremely talented performers making light work of the tenor line. These are the nice guys and gals – meek, mild, even-tempered individuals, consequently the butt of many orchestral jokes. Typical of these are:-

Question 1: What's the range of a viola?
Answer: As far as one can throw it.

Question 2: What's the coldest thing on earth after a polar bear's bottom?
Answer: A viola solo.

Many orchestral cellists seem not to occupy planet earth on a permanent basis but appear rather as visitors from elsewhere – most likely Planet Cello. They are often the most affected bunch in the orchestra, renowned for such antics as swaying about, shaking their heads and pulling the strangest of faces. In the nicest sense, they are the sworn enemies of the bass section for (a) dumping their cello cases in the spot where the basses sit and (b) immediately after rehearsal has started shuffling their chairs backwards enmasse, causing the basses to retreat backwards, resulting in the bass players ending up burning their backs on the hot wall radiators. Bass players have a favourite joke about the cello tribe:

Question: How does one know when the cellos are playing out of tune?
Answer: One can see their bows moving.

Now to the double bass section – but of course after many long years in the section I'm biased and possibly an unreliable witness. The bass section is the foundation of the entire orchestral edifice, tonally and rhythmically, and it is this section which really should drive the orchestra, and equally importantly, steady it in a rocky passage. Without a decent bass section the orchestra is the equivalent of a ship without a rudder. From time to time the section forms alliances with the brass, percussion and bassoons, the latter particularly in baroque and early classical compositions. Bass players are usually happy extrovert characters, but paradoxically deep thinkers! They become resigned over the years to hearing supposedly funny comments such as:-

"How do you manage to get that under your chin?"
"By heck, you must have fed that fiddle well."

If I had a fiver every time I'd heard just those two, by now I'd have built up a huge pension fund.

Members of woodwind section are the resident soloists of the orchestra, they are the flute (and piccolo), oboe, clarinet and to a lesser extent the bassoon, the bass voice of the family. They have a tendency to exhibitionism in solo passages, but are viewed by other sections as a steady, reliable bunch, especially the bassoons. As individuals on permanent solo duty they have got to conquer nervousness - anything less than performance perfection and everyone notices. Perhaps one should excuse the occasional lapse towards exhibitionism. Personally, I've great admiration for their ability to produce the goods under continual pressure. Several extremely competent woodwind players have admitted to me that they do experience an attack of nerves before a concert, but these usually disappear as soon as the performance gets under way.

I feel completely at ease commenting on the brass section since in an earlier orchestral life, I laboured as a trombonist for some three years. To many people the brass section represents the boozy branch of the orchestra – a reputation not entirely undeserved. Toward the end of a performance, these players often harbour too many thoughts about getting to the bar before the rush to play reliably. However in their defence, their part is truly exposed and the potential for a total disaster looms large, and it's no wonder many fancy a drink or three. With the exception of the French Horns known in musical circles as horns, brass players generally are outward looking, extrovert characters. In contrast horn players tend to neurosis, by the very nature of the instrumental difficulties they face. Quite rightly is the horn regarded as the queen of the orchestra. However given the ease of 'splitting' notes, hitting a wrong harmonic in the closely spaced series and often having to transpose at sight, it's no wonder that as a sub-branch they are everlasting worriers.

My admiration for the skill and sheer courage of percussionists knows no bounds. Mistakes or hesitancy by these individuals can ruin a performance and what's more the audience can see it, hear it, and knows it. Percussionists standing as they do in an elevated position at the rear of the orchestra in full view of the audience, are on a hiding to nothing. Their bravery, or possible foolhardiness, is unequalled in the orchestra. The fact that the percussionist has simply to hit something, and with the exception of the timpanist is unconcerned about intonation, leads most people to believe their job is an easy one. Quite the contrary, they have to endure long periods of inactivity, and their ability not to miscount runs of a hundred bars rest, is the first hazard to overcome.

In relation to bars rest, I'm reminded of the story of Sir Thomas Beecham who during a rehearsal cued the cymbal player for his entry. The cymbal remained silent. Sir Thomas stopped the orchestra and repeated from a few bars back with the same result. The same routine happened a couple more times. An exasperated Sir Thomas finally addressed the cymbalist *"Mr Cymbal, you're missing 18 bars after letter G." "Nothing to clash for bars ahead, sir,"* came the reply. Sir Thomas, quick as a flash retorted *"Look my man, when I point at you then you jolly well clash those cymbals, otherwise I look a bloody fool."*

The percussionist also requires an impeccable sense of timing and rhythm. Given that a mistake hasn't occurred in counting bars rest, the percussionist's strike has to be delivered with the split second accuracy – anything less and the dramatic effect is spoiled. Finally, the percussionist has to be adept at flitting between various pieces of percussion kit, with the potential for a disaster of gigantic proportions. A trip and the ultimate indignity of dropping the cymbals onto the stage floor with a loud clatter, is every percussionists' nightmare. Truly, members of this section are the kamikazes of the musical world!

There is one solitary instrument, which although technically a string instrument, is never included in the string section of the orchestra. The instrument in question is the harp and since there's usually only one of them, it would hardly qualify as an orchestra section. Just occasionally there maybe more than one harp deployed, in which case it would be reasonable to refer to a harp section. Symphonie Fantastique by Berlioz scored for two harps is probably the instance best known to most regular concertgoers. The notion that the harp is an orchestral misfit is strengthened by the fact that the list of players at the back of a concert programme does not include the harpist's name amongst the strings, but it usually appears after the percussionists' names – appearing almost as an afterthought. Harpists, usually ladies, are independent creatures and most freelance in the amateur world, rarely becoming permanent orchestra members.

Every orchestra has a conductor. It is over 70 years ago that I played my first symphony concert and I've still to find out why! Joking aside, these individuals at the highest level are often paid vast sums, so the musical establishment must believe they add some value. The concert going public, who only see them on the podium at the concert, possibly doesn't realise that their main work has already been completed during the allotted rehearsal schedule. I've never canvased the opinions of my playing colleagues to ask what they think is important in a conductor, but hearing their comments over the years has given me a fair idea.

Whatever else, the conductor must turn up at the rehearsal with a detailed knowledge of the orchestral score and have a clear idea of the interpretation he or she requires. This is not as difficult as it sounds, for nowadays there are probably a host of recordings of the work being studied. The conductor should not be afraid to make subtle musical changes during the rehearsal schedule to highlight that particular orchestra's strengths or to cover a certain weakness. To achieve this end the conductor must have excellent communication skills, not simply oral ones but a body language which can be read by all the players. Many conductors have a bad habit of turning towards the first violins when addressing the orchestra, resulting in the situation that the back desks of the cellos and the bass section can't hear the instruction/comment, and are completely at a loss where perhaps a repeat is to be taken from.

On the question of repeatedly rehearsing a particular passage *'to get it right'*, there is absolutely no point in pursuing that procedure unless the conductor can point out precisely what the problem is, and how it might be solved. Repeating the passage simply reinforces the *'mistake'* or problem. Orchestral players look to the conductor to provide a clear beat, and hope that the various tempi set in rehearsal are followed in performance. Some conductors I've known have had a tendency to speed up at a performance, no doubt as a result of an adrenalin rush. Can the orchestra manage without conductor for a performance?
A professional orchestra can cope well, after the conductor has started the piece. The orchestra I play with regularly now, the Cardiff Phiharmonic Orchestra (CPO), an amateur yet near professional standard orchestra, has also demonstrated that on many occasions in rehearsal. Conductor Michael Bell

having started the piece, has wandered off into the auditorium to hear what it sounded like - the orchestra continued to play unhindered!!

Perhaps the most famous story of an orchestra carrying on a performance without a conductor is that of the Vienna Philharmonic playing Beethoven's Eroica symphony at The Musikverein under Karl Boehm. The lights failed half way through the final movement, the players knew it by heart and simply carried on. Near the end the audience heard a woodwind player ask in a loud voice (referring to Boehm), *"is he still here or has he gone home?"*

But it is not just technical ability which marks out a good conductor, but personality is equally important. I have been appalled to read from time to time the overbearing and downright rudeness displayed by some great named conductors. This would never happen in the amateur ranks where the players simply would not put up with such behaviour – they are not being paid and would simply walk away. I always smile when I think of an incident when the great conductor Koussivitsky, noted for his notoriously short fuse, dismissed a player on the spot. On his way out the player walked past the maestro and remarked *"Nuts to you"*. Koussevitsky, as quick as a flash replied, *"It's too late to apologise."* Conductors of amateur orchestras need to be quite firm but at the same time friendly, and an encouraging word together with a spot of praise where merited never goes amiss.

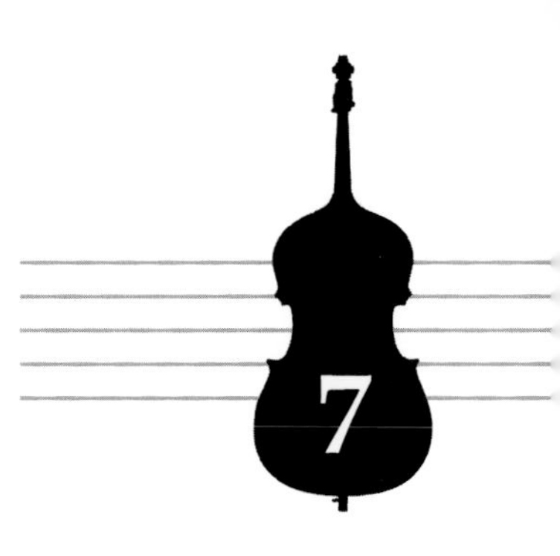

Elation, Calm, Boredom, Terror

What is it really like to play in an orchestra?
That question has been asked of me many times. Leaving aside for a moment the emotional aspects, much depends on the physical environment where the concert is taking place.

A nice bright modern air-conditioned concert hall, with good clean facilities for changing into concert dress, certainly inspires confidence and gives a feeling of well-being, allowing the player to relax - well, at least a bit. On the subject of changing facilities and locations I've endured over the years, some have been almost bizarre. How about, in a public toilet, behind gravestones in a churchyard, in a school corridor, in a farm barn, behind the bushes, in a moving bus? Of course, unisex ones can create hilarious situations as might be imagined. The most memorable location occurred under the pulpit of a church in Switzerland when on tour with the CPO in 1996.

Lighting is also extremely important for the notes on the part and other markings such as accidentals are the very devil to spot in gloomy surroundings. The strange dots representing ill-formed notes and many miscellaneous abbreviations which often crop up on manuscript parts, are often almost impossible to sight read in poor lighting.

Perhaps the most trying and sometimes depressing venues, are churches and cathedrals. These are often cold, draughty places with dreadful lighting. Many times the area available between the chancel and the nave for setting out the orchestra music stands, incidentally always referred to as 'desks' in the trade, is small and awkwardly shaped. The matter becomes pressing if a choir has to be accommodated nearby. The restricted space often causes some strange seatings, for instance where the trombone section ends up amongst the violas and the tuba alongside the flutes. Many times I've had my bass jammed hard up against a massive gothic pillar, which has left my desk partner and myself hardly any bowing room.

Space restriction in churches and cathedrals reminds me of a concert in Llandaff Cathedral some years ago with the CPO when this issue caused a minor panic in the bass section. The basses were seated in two rows, one behind the other, consequently the rear rank partially blocked a side aisle. On duty during rehearsal was a young, officious Verger with a none-too Christian attitude. Several times he came along and insisted the aisle be kept completely clear. We pointed out politely that we simply couldn't achieve the ideal, but at least there was still a passage, although restricted, for people to pass. Despite being continually harassed by him throughout the rehearsal, the section stood its ground. We returned for the evening performance to discover that all of the section's music stands and parts had mysteriously disappeared. Panic searches failed to locate this vital equipment and it was not until seconds before the conductor Mike Bell was due to appear on the podium that the verger announced with a smirk that he'd discovered these hidden away in one of the cupboards. Suspicious or what?

Returning to the question of the emotional aspects experienced when playing in an orchestra. This is most likely what the questioners had in mind when asking me the question. Of course, I can only answer this from a personal viewpoint. For me, elation, inner calm, sheer terror and boredom sum it up nicely. As a bass player, belting out the bottom line in a forte passage of Beethoven or Brahms symphony gives me a feeling of immense elation. Incidentally, Brahms's dad earned his living as a bass player in Hamburg and it seems that he must have passed a few hints on to his young lad of the sort of bass line likely to do it for bass players. In experiencing such a high, one has to be on guard against becoming too enthusiastic and losing concentration. After all, concentration is everything when performing.

Certain works induce a feeling of relaxed inner calm. The slow movements of many major symphonies and concertos induce this feeling and one has to be vigilant that one doesn't drift off, particularly in a few bars rest, and suddenly find the section had started playing half a bar ago. For me, Nimrod from Elgar's Enigma Variations is very emotional and so beautiful to play I could almost cry. I'm also similarly affected by the slow movement of the Beethoven violin concerto.

Sheer terror fortunately doesn't occur too frequently, but when it does one begins to sweat a bit and in extreme circumstances the bowing arm is difficult to control. It usually arises when there is a tricky exposed passage looming a few bars ahead which during rehearsal, created terrible problems and success on the night is by no means certain. Sometimes negative thoughts about the tricky passage creep in even when playing pieces earlier in the concert programme. In circumstances where the awkward passage went well it is easy to imagine the great relief and relaxation afterwards.

Boredom of course should never occur but frequently does. For bass players, Ravel's Bolero must the most boring piece ever written. Bar after bar of the same mind numbing repetitiveness, it's hard not to lose count of the repeating bars. The instrumental cues on the part are not much help either. Rehearsals at times can be boring, particularly when long practice periods are devoted to other sections of the orchestra. In these circumstances it's not unknown for the smart phones to suddenly appear, and a spot of surreptitious texting to take place.

Going on tour away from the orchestra's main base can be a tiring, yet usually a fun experience, with a golden opportunity for players to 'let their hair down' when off duty. It allows players the chance of a little light hearted banter and also to get to know their colleagues better, particularly those from other sections. Few amateur orchestras undertake such a commitment, because either their standard is such that they would be unable to draw an audience without support of friends and family or the logistics of making tour arrangements is simply too onerous. The tours may simply be a one day performance in a venue within a reasonable travelling distance of base, whilst others may be several days away.

The CPO has played many one-day engagements out of Cardiff. Concerts in Monmouth, Brecon, Blackwood, Pembroke, Porthcawl, Neath, Narberth and Tenby have been undertaken in recent years, some of those being regular annual engagements.

Weekend tours have also featured in the CPO schedule with concerts in the Hall for Cornwall in Truro being presented on a Sunday afternoon. Travel has occupied the previous morning and early afternoon, with an evening concert on that day in either Exeter or Plymouth. Although these tours were enjoyable, the downside was the long return haul arriving back in Cardiff late at night.

Continental tours have been a feature of life in the CPO since 1996 when the orchestra undertook a three concert tour of Switzerland. France beckoned two years later with three concerts in Evereux, Tours and Paris. For me personally, to be performing at the Salle Pleyel Paris the French equivalent of The Royal Albert Hall, was one of the outstanding memories of my musical career. The programme that evening was Bernstein's Candide Overture, Grace William's Fantasia on Welsh Nursery Tunes, Rachmaninov's Symphony No.2, and Saint-Saen's Violin Concerto No.3 with the young soloist Raki Singh. At the end of the programme the audience called for an encore and we obliged with The Farandol from Bizet's L'Arlesienne Suite. Outside the hall's main entrance was a painted board listing the dates and the orchestras performing in the venue that season. We knew CPO had truly arrived on the music scene when our name and date was displayed on the painted board outside the main entrance between that of the Berlin Philharmonic and the Vienna Philharmonic.

As a result of that success the CPO was invited to play the final concert of the British Millennium Festival in Paris's magnificent Eglise de la Madelaine, where Saint-Saens and Faure had been organists. I will for ever remember the final fortissimo D minor chord of Bach's Toccata and Fugue (arranged for orchestra by Stowkowski) with which we opened that concert. The echo must have taken 15 seconds to die away. CPO's last visit to France was in 2007 to play two concerts at Cardiff's twin city of Nantes.

With a live music performance there are no second chances, you either get it right or you don't. Of course there are degrees of 'rightness', but it is this constant pressure to achieve perfection which can place the orchestral player under enormous psychological stress. A tough mental attitude can help and in this regard musicians have much in common with sporting types, golfers and snooker players in particular, and with actors. The extent to which it is possible to get away with a mistake or a spot of loose playing depends on the particular instrument and what else is happening in the score at the time. A bit of dodgy intonation by a second fiddler during the final part of the 1812 Overture or the fourth movement of Respighi's Pines of Rome is hardly likely to be noticed in the clamour of the brass going full belt and supported by a massive percussion section. Poor intonation or a duff note from a woodwind or horn soloist in a quiet passage, and everyone knows!

On many occasions I've shared a desk with a professional. It goes without saying that technically, these individuals are outstanding as one would expect with conservatoire training – and being paid for doing the job. Their initial study and relentless practice, often starting in their pre-teenage years, is then often followed by an apprenticeship at the back of the bass section or as a freelance. However, if I were to choose two outstanding qualities which mark out the professional, first it would be their ability to concentrate yet at the same time to appear entirely relaxed. Second is their uncanny accuracy, not just in terms of note length, style, dynamic, timing, bow management etc, but particularly their intonation. Believe me, they don't often play out of tune. Just to show they are human after all, one hopes that from time to time they might make a mistake!

Despite their undoubted skills, professional orchestral musicians are in my view, seriously underpaid. In what other profession do members begin their studies often well before they have reached their teenage years? From thereon there is no let-up either, what with working for grades, competitions and auditions, all of which require considerable effort and dedication. What's even worse, I can't think of another profession (except possible airline pilots) where regular demanding tests are required to simply stay in post. Many orchestras audition their players, and any deemed as failures are placed on warnings or in the worst cases, dismissed. Even despite all the uncertainty, the pool of young talent doing the rounds of auditions seeking a permanent professional orchestral position, is huge. Somehow, that just doesn't make sense – or am I missing something?

8

Music - A Dangerous Occupation

"Sorry, but I'm afraid an operation is the only answer." Those were the words ringing in my ears after I'd been examined in the consulting room of the orthopaedic surgeon. *"It's a relatively straightforward procedure"* the man in the white coat assured me, despite its fearsome sounding name, Sub-Acromial Decompression. Quite simply he was proposing to remove a chunk of bone from my right shoulder, the one that the bowing arm connects to, in order to relieve the pressure on the tendon. *"Can I have it done under a local?"* I asked tentatively. *"No way, it's a general, or it doesn't get done,"* was the firm uncompromising response.

Almost 60 years of bass playing had finally taken its toll, but more specifically I blame Handel for it. A couple of years previously when somewhat out of practice, I'd played a Messiah for the Mountain Ash Choral Society. The great man himself is rather cruel to bass players and in this work he hardly gives us a bar rest. The gig was a three hour afternoon rehearsal followed by the two hour evening concert. It turned out that I was the only bass engaged, so with my respect for Handel I'd given it some *'welly'* in the big choruses. I knew the very next day that I'd done myself a mischief, for the shoulder pain was excruciating and over the next few days it didn't improve. In fact it got worse to the extent that I could no longer move my arm. I struggled for the next year or so with the medical profession prescribing a vast array of treatments, all to no avail. Cash spent on physiotherapy also failed to get near the problem and in the end I was reduced to trying all manner of folk remedies and concoctions from health food shops. The short answer was that I had simply wasted my time and more importantly, money. What's more, my playing career had virtually ceased with only the occasional lightweight concert during that period. What two years of NHS treatment and my own ineffective medical efforts had failed to achieve, was put right by crossing a man's hand with silver for a forty five minute operation.

The recovery was a longish process which gave me ample time to reflect on my unfortunate circumstances, and to undertake research on my fellow musicians' injuries. What a weird and wonderful set of ailments potentially beset my colleagues. I bet if some of them had known the dangers before embarking on an instrumentalist's career, they'd have taken up kick boxing, wrestling, sky diving, hang gliding or bungee jumping instead.

The composer Jean-Baptiste Lully (b. Florence, 1632, d. Paris 1687) had the misfortune to die as a result of a musical accident sustained whilst conducting a performance of his Te Deum. He was beating time using a heavy pole with which to hit the floor. Unfortunately, his aim was somewhat haphazard and he struck himself on the big toe. The toe became gangrenous, which in the days before antibiotics had extremely serious consequences. The only certain treatment was amputation and this he refused. He is the only case I'm aware of where man died for his musical art. I'm sure there must be others whose demise has passed unrecorded. Fortunately, musical ailments generally don't end in the extreme manner of Lully, although sometimes the effects can be quite serious, and certainly depressing for the players concerned.

Making music might be good for the soul - but according to a research paper *'Contact dermatitis and other skin conditions in instrumental musicians'* by Thilo Gambichler, Stefanie Bom and Marcus Freitag published as recently as 2004 in the respected journal BMC Dermatology, confirms that it can be seriously bad for the skin. Prolonged contact with the instrument can trigger unpleasant dermatological conditions. Whilst not wishing to frighten my colleagues, the authors reported on a wide range of recognised medical conditions such as Fiddler's Neck, Guitar Nipple, Flautist's Chin and Clarinetist's Cheilitis – no, I'm not joking! Cellists, in particular, are at considerable risk of succumbing to a range of afflictions, amongst them Cellist's Chest, Cellist's Knee, and presumably most painful and embarrassing of all for male cellists, Cello Scrotum – more on the latter condition later in this chapter.

Apart from musculoskeletal problems (e.g. tendosynovitis) and neurological disorders (e.g. focal dystonia) instrumental musicians are a high risk group for a variety of skin conditions, since an intense contact between the instrument and the performer's skin is usually necessary during performance. Although not life threatening, they may lead to impaired performance and are a definite occupational hazard.

A range of adverse factors has been identified in certain specific instances. For example many case observations have reported on Fiddler's Neck, which manifests itself as an area of lichenification and hyperpigmentation (usually a red mark) on the side of the neck below the angle of the jaw on the side the violin is held. Erythema, scaling, cyst, and scar formation, papules and pustules and even focal neck oedema may occur at this location as well. With such a catalogue of potential nasties I'm surprised anyone would want to play the violin! On a lighter note, many lady violinists with the condition have reported receiving the look, which says *'I-know-what-you-were-up-to-last-night'*.

Reports have indicated that viola players are believed to be more prone to develop the condition than violinists because the instrument is larger and heavier. It has been suggested that local pressure gripping the violin or viola under the chin, friction, shearing stress and sensitivity to the chin rest, particularly where the ebony has been artificially blackened with 'Ursol-Echtschwarz' containing para-phenylenediamine, are all factors triggering the allergic reaction.

You would think that the newspaper headline *'Orchestral Musicians Have Poor Hearing'* is a joke. Not so! The recent case of the viola player Chris Goldscheider suing his employers the Royal Opera House for ruining his hearing and his career has highlighted a real problem, particularly for professional musicians. Court documents suggest that his position in the orchestra immediately in front of the brass section during rehearsals for Wagner's Die Walkure exposed him to a peak noise level of 137 decibels (dB), equivalent to the level of a jet engine [at what distance is not specified]. The effect on the human hearing is to create a permanent traumatic threshold shift which causes the brain to amplify day-to-day sounds. That this hearing impairment is not an isolated case is confirmed in a large scale study published in the journal Occupational & Environmental Medicine, which reported that musicians were 4 times more likely to develop noise-induced hearing loss compared to non-musicians. It is not simply the seating position in the orchestra which may cause hearing problems, but worryingly the proximity of the instrument to its player. Flutes can reach 112dB, the tiny piccolo 120dB, whilst a violinist's left ear can be subjected to 100dB sound emanating from the f-hole. Aren't we bass players lucky to have the f-hole a long way from our ears and also to be seated on the periphery of the orchestra sideways on to the brass section?

Until recently cellists were thought to be subject to the triple whammy referred to above. However lady cellists could overcome their major chest problem with the use of suitably padded bra. For years, my mind boggled at exactly how a male cellist could end up with Cellist's Scrotum. Although there's no accounting for taste, I did wonder if some male cellists actually took their instrument to bed. However, the many fanciful theories which have been advanced over the years to explain this condition are now simply redundant. The condition is a hoax! This hoax is not on the scale of Piltdown Man but a complete hoax nevertheless, which has taken in some of the best brains in the country just as Piltdown Man did for over half a century.

In 2009 it was revealed that cello scrotum was dreamed up in 1974 by John Murphy and Elaine Murphy (now Baroness Murphy). The letter from John Murphy, published in the British Medical Journal, was in response to a previously published letter from a Dr Curtis regarding skin irritation which the latter had observed among classical guitarists. The Murphys thought it highly likely that the Curtis letter was a spoof and decided to go one better by pretending to have noted a similar phenomenon amongst male cellists. To their amazement, the letter was published and it was in this manner that cello scrotum entered the learned discourse of the medical profession. Of course, we'll never know how many males have been put off taking up the cello as a result of this spurious condition.

Many string players have allergic reactions resulting from contact with metal strings of the iron-chromium alloy type which has had nickel added to increase the resistance to corrosion and pitting. It is the nickel component which triggers the reaction and this metal is also the root cause of Flautist's Chin. Metal flutes contain a proportion of nickel in the alloy from which the flute is made, and contact between the instrument and the lower lip and chin causes some players to develop this irritation. Brass players also have been known to suffer from allergic reactions from parts of instruments which have been nickel plated.

Whilst not wishing to alarm my trumpet and horn playing colleagues, both groups can additionally be afflicted with what sounds to be distressing conditions. In the former case 'Satchmo's syndrome' which is a rupture of the orbicularis oris, has been recorded. The poor horn player may suffer from a circumscribed atrophy of the upper lip as well as ischaemia of the lips. However, of far more significance to these players is Brass Player's Ale Gut. Onset is due to too many pieces being marked Tacet, coupled with close proximity to bars of the non-musical variety. Abstinence is the only certain cure.

There are many other materials associated with musical instruments which give rise to allergic reactions. In the case of string instruments, ebony fingerboards have been known to cause an allergic reaction, particularly if these have been stained. Varnish containing propolis cera and widely used on string instruments, has been reported as a cause of allergic reactions. Rosin derived from conifer trees contains a complex mixture of acids and natural substances. Rosin is applied to the bow to provide a bit of 'bite'. The complex rosin has been shown to be a cause of allergic reactions in string players. Cane reeds have also come under suspicion in cases where woodwind players have had allergic reactions. However, Clarinettist's Cheilitis is more likely to be caused by a combination of factors including friction, local intense pressure on the lower lip, shearing and occlusion. Distressing as allergic reactions can be, there are many other occupational hazards which players should be aware of.

Bassoonist's Tongue is a very painful condition and first presents as a blister on the tip of the tongue due to striking the end of the reed repeatedly. Eventually the blister bursts and a bleeding open wound results. I know first hand by observing my daughter's determined practice to achieve a distinction at Grade 8 on this instrument, just how painful and depressing this condition can be. I'm told that a palliative is to avoid rapid articulation, and in extreme cases stop playing and hum the part.

Cymbal Player's Vibration is a troublesome condition suffered by lady percussionists when having to stop a clashed pair of cymbals vibrating, using the nearest sticking out part of their anatomy. This condition becomes acute in pieces like Tchaikovsky's 4th symphony where repeated loud clashes are demanded, and may explain why lady percussionists avoid playing the cymbals if at all possible.

Bass Player's Syndrome is a whole raft of ailments associated with playing this most dangerous of instruments. It is almost certain that during their careers, bass players will be affected by one or more of the conditions. Pizzicato features frequently in bass parts, and prolonged forte passages of this technique result in blistered fingers. Some jazz performers tape the finger ends to avoid the problem altogether. Bass strings are thick, heavy beasts. For example, the thickest on a 4 string bass is the E string, which is 2.7mm in diameter compared with the equivalent violin's G string of 0.7mm diameter. Although the action (the height of the strings above the fingerboard) can be varied to suit particular players' preferences they are nevertheless several mm higher than other members of the string family. The finger pressure required to stop the massive heavy strings onto the fingerboard is considerable in the case of the bass and it is little wonder that bass players develop painful arthritis of the left hand finger joints. After a lifetime of bass playing the fingers of my left hand are now totally deformed, in particular the index finger which is most frequently used, and the naturally weak little finger. I know several players who dose themselves regularly on Ibuprofen which affords some relief. Repetitive Strain Injury (RSI) is yet another hazard, but fortunately bass parts don't usually contain the long fast semi quaver runs of the fiddles, viola and cello sections, consequently the risk to us is that much less. The thickness and length of the bass strings demands considerable bow weight particularly in forte passages, and a strong right arm is a pre-requisite for bass players. However in extreme cases, torn ligaments, tendons and muscles of the arm and shoulder can be the outcome of a prolonged forte bowing campaign – much as I discovered to my cost! Bass players tend to suffer from bad backs too, mainly caused by lugging around a heavy instrument, often exacerbated by an awkward seating position. I know of one veteran bass player who was having back and neck trouble. He consulted his doctor, who discovered that his right shoulder was considerably lower than his left. This was entirely due to carrying his bass on his back for many years with the strap always passing over his right shoulder, the latter bearing the full weight of the bass. Oh dear, what we bass players have to endure! Medical specialists ought to recommend sensible people should avoid this instrument at all costs!

Moving to keyboard instruments, Pianist's Thumb is an affliction resulting from too many glissandos which damage the thumbnail, and sometimes cause terrible pain in the thumb joint. Restricting the repertoire to Baroque and Classical is the medical profession's sound advice.

Still with the keyboard (and pedals), Organist's Trousers is not a true medical condition but simply a shiny trouser seat, caused by sliding about on the organ bench when pedalling. I'm reliably informed that this condition has the advantage of allowing tax relief to be claimed on replacements.

Second Fiddler's Intonation Malaise which again is not a true medical condition, had alarming, possibly even life threatening consequences for one individual second fiddler some years ago. The story is apocryphal and concerns the highly regarded Italian maestro Victor de Sabata (1892-1967), who was nicknamed de Sabotage. According to the story De Sabata had 3 main attributes: a very keen ear, a ferocious temper, and reputedly a wooden leg, which on one occasion he used with devastating effect. Following several unsuccessful attempts to rectify the poor intonation of one unfortunate second violinist who his keen ear had identified, De Sabata strode over to the offending player, detached his leg and hit him over the head with it rendering him senseless. He rejoined himself to his leg and, on his way back to the podium was heard to mutter loudly, *"the problem is solved."*

9

Red Faces All Round

By their very nature, amateur orchestras have the potential for almighty *'cock-ups'*. Eighty or so players from diverse backgrounds and of varying musical abilities are hardly the homogenous group which professional orchestras represent, musically at least. That is not to say that from time to time the professionals don't get it wrong – they do occasionally, but their playing is far more secure and their position on the disaster scale is naturally that much lower.

Simply to assemble eighty characters in the venue and onto the platform for a rehearsal or concert on time is a feat in itself. I remember an incident some years ago with the City of Cardiff Symphony Orchestra when a scheduled rehearsal prior to a concert never took place. The orchestra was booked to perform, along with a male voice choir and soloists at a sports centre in New Tredegar in South Wales's Rhymney Valley. Several of the orchestra myself included, had driven to the hall in our own cars and as a group we were hanging around chatting and awaiting the arrival of the coach bringing the majority of players. The scheduled start time of 3pm passed with neither sight nor sound of the bus contingent. We were beginning to question if we'd turned up on the right day when this doubt was settled by the arrival of the male choir, who entertained us for the rest of the afternoon by rehearsing their 'solo' numbers. Teatime arrived but still no sign of the lost souls, so we wandered off to a local workingmen's club for a pie and a pint. On returning to the hall about an hour or so before kick off, our spirits were lifted by the sight of a coach. The driver had mistakenly driven to the town of Tredegar in the adjacent Sirhowy Valley. There the fugitives undertook a lengthy, fruitless search to find the hall before the penny finally dropped. New Tredegar and Tredegar are only some 5miles apart as the crow flies, but to get from one to the other involves a circuitous route approaching 20 miles on somewhat indifferent roads. Needless to say the concert went ahead without a rehearsal!

A catastrophic and embarrassing start to a concert occurred about 30 years ago in St. Woolos Cathedral, Newport, South Wales. I was playing with the St. Woolos Chamber Orchestra, a scratch band assembled for occasional concerts held mainly in the Cathedral. The programme that evening was one in which the orchestra performed a few classical and baroque compositions and also accompanied the Cathedral Choir. I recall that one of the pieces in which we accompanied the choir was the Anthem *'Rejoice in the Lord Alway'*, an unusual departure from the customary organ accompaniment. The audience was a sizeable one and was waiting expectedly for the concert to begin. The orchestra members were in their places and ready for action – apart from the occupants of the two first fiddle desks, who were nowhere to be seen. The conductor now on the podium, became agitated, and from time to time he glanced furtively towards the vestry, willing the players of the top line to appear. After a delay of what seemed like several minutes, four completely flustered ladies in concert dress burst in, hurriedly sat down, and placed their parts on the music stands. Without further delay, the conductor gave the downbeat – a total disaster ensued. The four first fiddles commenced playing the wrong piece! Unbeknown to them the programme running order had been changed at the last minute. In their confusion they had even failed to spot the two instrumental soloists, instruments poised, standing in front of the orchestra ready to give the concert a flamboyant start with Vivaldi's *Concerto in C* for 2 Trumpets. The explanation for their tardiness lay in the fact that they had travelled to the concert in one car and arrived at the last minute. They were then unable to park in the vicinity of the Cathedral as there is not much parking available in any event, but especially on a concert night.

With an orchestra large or small, I'm amazed things don't go wrong more often since there's a universe of potential pitfalls. Sometimes when things do go adrift they are of a minor nature known only to the offending player, and perhaps to colleagues seated nearby. At the other extreme are the real howlers, which even those hard of hearing in the audience would spot. Those are the ones which cause the red faces! If amateur players are being honest in this respect, and in most cases they usually are, I reckon all would admit to at least one *'clanger'* in their careers. In my case I've a few to confess.

Lack of concentration is responsible for more instrumental errors than any other cause. My absolute nightmare resulting from a momentary lapse happened at a Spring Brass Band Contest at Belle Vue, Manchester in the 1950's. I was playing in the Grand Shield competition, the top section out of six, in the Kings Hall. This venue had a stage in the centre, usually used for boxing or wrestling matches surrounded on all sides by rising, tiered seating holding an audience of over 2,000. During our performance of the test piece in front of a packed audience, I boldly blew a double forte C, which is right in the middle of the trombone's range. The problem was it was in a silent bar! The note rang out loud and clear – I could almost hear the audience gasp. Oh, how I wished the floor could have swallowed me up. Such is my shame, I cannot even remember the test piece and I'll not embarrass the band by naming it. The adjudicators I do remember were Edward Buttress and William Scholes. Clearly, they were kind, sympathetic men who apparently ignored this technical faux pas on my part, and their written remarks even complimented the trombone section on its performance.

You wouldn't believe that total concentration can also lead to error. It has happened to me a couple of times and other string players have told me that they have been similarly affected. The problem always arises at the start of a piece, often the opening number of the concert or the one immediately following the interval. At that point one concentrates very hard indeed, having checked the correct finger has been put down at the correct position on the correct string, one is then totally absorbed in watching and waiting for the conductor's downbeat. This eventually arrives and lo and behold one somehow manages to bow the wrong string. With a bit of luck, it's a double forte opening for the entire orchestra and so the error passes un-noticed.

A faulty technique is a frequent source of error and in my case this led to an embarrassing incident early in my brass band career. In mitigation it wasn't with the trombone, but the one and only time I've been a percussionist. My first band Clayton West, always toured the village playing carols on Christmas Day and Boxing Day, a tradition which now sadly seems to have died out. A pause at the Woodman Inn with landlord Billy Hawke serving a round of free drinks, and with two later stops at the Junction and Shoulder of Mutton pubs, together with drinks provided at several houses on our travels, ensured that by mid-afternoon most were feeling what may best be described as exuberant. One Boxing Day at a halt in High Street, our bass drummer blacksmith Bert Swanick, needed to leave the scene for necessary relief. I took over the bass drum duty. Even though it was mid afternoon, Hail Smiling Morn was a popular request. It is a rousing 6/8 melody, which allowed ample opportunity for me to show off my newly acquired bass drum skills. By the second verse I was hitting the drum hard at 2 beats to the bar when, to my absolute horror, I lost my grip on the drumstick. I could only look on anxiously as it described a beautiful arc through the air and disappeared under a passing No. 15 Yorkshire Traction bus on its way to Barnsley. Much to my relief it wasn't smashed to matchwood under the wheels, nor had it lodged on the bus' underside to end up in Barnsley bus station. I put the drum down on the road and made off to recover the stick only to find the drum rolling away down the hill. I sprinted off after the run-away drum and caught it just before it mounted the pavement, thus preventing it smashing into a stone wall. Sheepishly, I returned to recover the stick and realized in that instant that percussionists are the kamikazes of the musical world.

Sometimes a combination of circumstances outside the control of the performer conspires to produce a red face situation. A rather bizarre moment happened to me in one of the early Welsh Philharmonic Orchestra (WPO) concerts in the early 1980's at Swansea's Brangwyn Hall. It was a mid-week concert in the height of summer and despite it being evening, the temperature was still hovering in the eighties. Chatting and wandering back onto the stage after the interval I was rather too liberal applying Nymans rosin to the bow hair. Nymans is noted as a sticky rosin and particularly so in hot weather. I seated myself on my bass stool and after tuning, placed the point of the bow on the A string ready to play a B natural, the opening note of Schubert's Symphony No. 8 in B Minor (The Unfinished). Just at that moment there was a bit of a commotion as a group of late arrivals vacating the bar were rejoining the audience. The conductor Alan Good, waited for possibly about a minute for the hall to settle before giving the downbeat. The opening is a very soft, almost mystical phrase shared by the cellos and basses. Starting on an up bow, I pushed the bow gently. The bow wouldn't move. The rosin had welded the bow hair to the string. In the heat of the moment some split seconds later I panicked, and pushed harder and harder. Suddenly the bow let go and the sound of a forte pizzicato type B natural echoed round the hall. The conductor Alan Good looked startled, and he clearly couldn't work out where this errant note had originated. The rest of the section never let on and I guess he's still as puzzled as ever, if he still remembers the incident.

On another occasion in 1986 at the Brangwyn Hall it was the concert promoters who suffered the red faces. The final piece of the WPO concert was Tchaikovsky's 1812 overture and during the afternoon rehearsal we had been told to expect massive loud bangs to simulate cannon fire during the final section. Unbeknown to the players the promoters had arranged for explosives contained in metal dustbins to be detonated in the entrance lobby. In the event the explosions were far more powerful than had been anticipated, even blowing the dustbins apart. The sound carried a huge distance and within 5 minutes the hall was surrounded by multitudes police, who imagined that the IRA, being very active in the 1980's, had undertaken a bombing campaign. Needless to say, the promoters were severely reprimanded and the evening performance had to make do with the percussion section doing its best with timps and bass drum.

Mis-counting bars rest by a player does not usually result in serious consequences for the whole orchestra. If a player's entry is late no-one other than the individual concerned and possibly colleagues alongside are aware of the error. A player is usually skilled enough to realise immediately the mistake of coming in early and so is able to at least partially conceal the error. However, I remember well a concert by the WPO on 22nd March 1987 at Theatr Elli, Llanelli when a mis-count of bars rest caused total chaos from which the orchestra had some difficulty in recovering. The piece was the Symphonie Fantastique by Berlioz and towards the end of the 4th movement (March to the Scaffold) the tubular bells have a prominent role. On this occasion the percussionist miscounted causing total confusion in the viola section, which has the next entry several bars later. Some viola players followed the incorrect tubular bells as their cue whilst others in the section who had counted their bars rest accurately made the correct entry. The problem was compounded when other sections in succession had to make a decision which of the two viola factions to follow. The shambles eventually sorted itself out avoiding a total breakdown.

As we have seen with the St. Woolos Orchestra earlier, rushing onto the platform at the last minute is not the best preparation for what is to follow. In fact, I'm aware of two further instances where this has resulted in red faces, as it happens both to woodwind players. The first occurred in the 1960's to Huddersfield Philharmonic Orchestra's principal clarinettist Tony Crowther. Tony, who was not short of a bob or two, rolled up to the venue at the last minute in his brand new E Type Jaguar (he was the first person I knew who owned one of these iconic cars). In the streets around the Town Hall it's difficult parking at the best of times, but on a concert night virtually impossible. He drove around for some time and eventually had to abandon his vehicle some distance away. By the time Tony scrambled onto the platform, tuning was almost finished and he had barely time to assemble the clarinet. This he did manage, but unfortunately he fixed the lower half of his A clarinet to the top half of his Bflat clarinet (or visa versa). I can't now recall the opening number, but Tony told me afterwards he realised immediately something was amiss with his instrument but several bars had elapsed before he figured out what it was.

A similar incident occurred to a flautist friend who had mistaken the concert's start time. He rushed onto the stage at the last minute, stuck his part on the stand and in his haste to meet the conductor's down beat failed to remove the cleaning rod from inside the instrument. Two bars in and he suddenly realised what had happened – fortunately no-one, other than the principal clarinettist and 2nd flute sitting either side were aware of his predicament.

Arriving on stage with plenty of time to spare certainly saved my friend Paul from a red face situation. He had been invited by principal trumpet Phil, (also a friend of many years standing) to try out with the CPO. Paul confidently took his seat on the platform at Cardiff's St. David's Hall but suddenly realised that he didn't recognise anyone else in the orchestra. He enquired from another in the trumpet section the whereabouts of Phil. The addressee looked puzzled and asked who Phil was and which orchestra he played with. On hearing the answer CPO, Paul received the shock news, *"this is the Royal Liverpool Philharmonic"*. Paul suddenly realised the CPO concert was in Llandaff Cathedral some 3 miles distant. He still made it to the rehearsal venue on time, and he and Phil are still doing a grand job in the CPO.

Which Musical Instrument?

I've often been asked which instrument is the easiest to play. The short answer is there isn't one. Without realising it, the questioner was really asking which instrument is quicker and easier to get started on and in so doing, is capable of producing a decent sound and maybe a simple tune. That's of course, an entirely different question. The recorder beloved of school children and their teachers springs to mind. In this case there is no awkward reed to control and no complicated keywork to cope with. The fingering is relatively easy to learn and it's simply a matter of careful tonguing and gentle blowing. If the recorder has been voiced correctly then with a modicum of good fortune a pleasant sound is the result. For that reason recorder groups have been the staple of practical music making in many junior schools for many years.

Likewise with a brass instrument it is not that difficult to obtain a passable sound and play reasonably in tune within a fairly short time. There are many youngsters tootling away quite happily on cornets, tenor horns, baritones and even euphoniums and tubas. The tuneful concerts by junior school bands formed by these youngsters are a source of great pleasure to parents and visitors at school fetes and open evenings. In contrast members of the string family are difficult to master in the initial stages. One has only to hear the efforts of the string sections of some school orchestras to realise that the unappealing sound, coupled with poor intonation, is a reflection of the instruments' difficulties during the learning stage. It's no wonder youngsters on these instruments are soon discouraged. Those who persevere ought to be awarded a medal!

However the apparent simplicity of some instruments and ease of sound production, rather obscures the true situation. With every musical instrument whether it is one as elementary in principle as the recorder, or some fiendishly complicated instrument, there are individuals out there who are prepared to devote hours of practice every day of their lives to reach the heights of perfection. These individuals set the gold standard for each instrument, and the matter of whether a particular instrument is easy to play is in this context, meaningless. This is not to deny the fact that certain instruments pose particular problems – problems which players often take years to resolve, if at all.

The choice of instrument is critical if some degree of success is to be achieved. First of all a person must be physically capable of coping with the chosen instrument. For example, in general it would be a significant disadvantage for a small, frail individual to be fancying the Bflat tuba. A bassoonist with small hands would also face problems from the outset. Similarly a bass player needs a reasonable hand span and pretty strong fingers. These are examples of obviously desirable and undesirable physical characteristics but there are others, which are far more subtle and not so readily observed. For instance a brass player's embouchure is of critical importance. It has an influence on the player's ability to play for extended periods and also on the quality of the sound produced. Tone production not only depends on the player's embouchure but also on the facial bone structure, and of the size, shape, nature and disposition of the air cavities in the head and chest. I have known brass players who are excellent instrumentalists otherwise, yet they have lacked that elusive superb sound despite having worked tirelessly towards that goal. There must be something lacking in their physical make-up. These latter elements cannot be assessed in advance, and it is a matter of luck whether a person has indeed the 'correct' attributes. In the case of most instruments, subtle factors outside the player's control can ultimately determine a player's success.

Of course it is not only a pre-requisite to be physically suited to the instrument but equally important are the psychological and emotional elements. Quite simply the player has to posses an overwhelming desire to play the chosen instrument. Long hard hours of relentless practice, multitudes of setbacks and disappointments await the budding instrumentalist. Without a genuine love for the instrument it is doubtful whether the enthusiasm for the inevitable long, solitary practice regime can be maintained. Is it any wonder that so many fall by the wayside?

It is important to realise at the outset that the choice will determine, to a large extent, the opportunities to participate in one or more of the wide variety of musical ensembles and musical genres. In the string instrument family, the double bass offers the widest range of opportunity being an essential member of the full, chamber and string orchestras, as well as having the opportunity to participate in the many forms of jazz and dance band ensembles. The remaining instruments of the string section are essentially limited to orchestral work only. However it is worth mentioning that the orchestral string section requires more players than the woodwind or brass sections, and it is therefore generally easier to obtain a position as a string player, the competition numerically being less severe. Furthermore as a woodwind or brass player it is far more difficult to cover up a mediocre performance. String players on the other hand can often hide away in the section and, provided they don't make glaring mistakes, can get away with 'faking it' in difficult passages.

Of the woodwind instruments, the clarinet has the widest range of opportunity, being an essential member of full and chamber orchestras. The clarinet is closely related to the saxophone family which is also in demand in jazz and dance bands. Therefore many clarinettists double on saxophone. The remaining members of the woodwind group, flutes, oboes and bassoons have little opportunity outside the orchestral context other than in military and wind bands, which are made up of a mixture of woodwind and brass instruments.

From the manifold brass instruments, the trombone and trumpet enjoy the widest scope being members of the full orchestra and on occasion, the chamber orchestra. Both instruments are also employed in the various forms of jazz and dance bands. Of course the brass band as its name suggests, is made up entirely of instruments in the brass family, excluding French horns. These range in pitch from the Bflat bass up to the Eflat soprano cornet and without doubt the vast majority of brass players are to be found in brass bands. Military bands also offer scope to players of these instruments.

Many times I've been asked what attributes are required for a person to become a reasonable orchestral bass player. I'm reminded of the story of a friend of mine who was the long serving principal bassist of a well-known professional northern orchestra. I was present at the time he was asked this very question by a serious, well spoken lady. The lady was a patron of the orchestra and was taking advantage of the opportunity offered after a subscription concert, to meet orchestra members for a cup of tea and a chat. My friend was completely taken aback, for apparently, he'd never faced this question. *"Well,"* he replied, *"one needs to have a sense of rhythm and timing – one needs excellent coordination - one needs a good ear to be able to play in tune - one needs to be able to read music accurately - one needs to listen and fit in with the rest of the band - one needs to be able to follow the conductor - one needs to be able to count bars rest - one needs to concentrate hard during performance."* The list went on - then as an after-thought, he added, mischievously, *"of course to play the bass it helps to be tone deaf."* The lady took it in good part and burst out laughing. At future subscription concerts she always sought out my friend and invariably enquired after his hearing! The list enumerated by my friend isn't that far wide of the mark for any orchestral instrumentalist.

From the above list probably the biggest worry for every instrumentalist irrespective of the type of music or ensemble in which they are participating, is that of intonation (playing in tune) – or, at least it should be. Anyone who claims they don't have such qualms is deluding themselves, or else in the words of Donald Rumsfeld *"they don't know they don't know."*

Double Bass – King of the Orchestral World

The double bass, despite being the largest orchestral instrument and on prominent display on the concert platform, is probably the least well known orchestral member and certainly, along with the viola the least well known of the string family. The reason is a simple one – rarely is it heard in a solo role.

From the perspective of the concert hall auditorium, one double bass looks much like any other. However, that is rather a long way from the truth. There is a much greater variation in shape and size than in any other member of the string instrument family.

Over the years there has been much discussion regarding the origin of the double bass, some writers believing it was a development of the bass viol due to it having similar sloping shoulders. Confusion has also arisen because players and writers over the centuries have used different names to describe the instrument. However, it is now generally accepted that it developed from the 16th century as a member of the violin family, and having the lowest sound. The word double in its title indicates that it *'doubles'* the bass line provided by the cello. In choral terminology the 1st and 2nd violins respectively provide the treble and alto lines, the viola the tenor line, and the cello the bass line. In the earlier baroque and classical periods the double bass simply played the bass line along with the cello, but pitched an octave below. Therefore it is easy to see the reason that the adjective *'double'* was attached to the term *'bass'*, to describe the lowest sounding string instrument. Indeed, today the instrument is still a transposing instrument because the sound is an octave below what is written in the music, although as bass players we never think of it in that manner.

There are two shapes or patterns to most double basses. One follows the traditional violin shape, although the shoulders (technically called upper bouts) are usually much narrower in proportion than those on violins, violas and cellos. This allows the player to assume a comfortable playing position particularly when reaching for higher positions on the fingerboard. The second form follows that of a viol, again with narrow shoulders but obviously omitting the 'corners' associated with the violin. There is no difference in playing technique between the two shapes.

In terms of size the difference is enormous, ranging from dinky chamber basses having a body length of about 85 cm, to monster German 5/4 models with a 120-125 cm body dimension. The most common size of bass played in present day orchestras is the 3/4 having a body length of about 111 cm. This is now considered a full size bass. The width of the instrument also displays considerable variation. When viewed directly from the front or back some instruments look emaciated. Others are generous in proportion and well rounded, reminiscent of the usual perception of Friar Tuck. Technically, the front and back are each divided into 3 sections called bouts. The bulbous lower section is named the lower bout, and by similar reasoning the upper section is the upper bout. The cutaway sections to prevent the bow hitting the body are referred to as C bouts, being approximately the shape of a letter C. On an average size 3/4 bass the lower bouts are about 67 cm wide, the upper around 52 cm and the C bouts 38 cm. However, there can be quite a variation in the upper bouts, for if this dimension is too wide then the higher positions on the finger board are awkward to achieve. Such basses are said to be 'difficult to get round'. Some instruments used for solo performances where considerable dexterity in the higher register is demanded have exaggerated sloping shoulders, totally unlike the generous cello shape. Many old basses in particular those sought after for solo work, have often had their shoulders cut down – apparently without detriment to the tone. The front and back are each glued to a strip right around the circumference known as the ribs. The rib depth i.e. the distance between the front and back, can vary from about 12cm to about 24 cm. The wider rib depths give a larger air volume inside the bass which allegedly provides a louder sound. Basses with the wide rib dimension can also be 'difficult to get round'.

The front of the bass, correctly called *'the table'*, but often referred to as *'the belly'* or *'the front'* is carved out of spruce. A closer and straighter grain is said to produce a superior tone, but in fact I have known basses with wobbly uneven grain often carrying knots to produce a delightful sound. The thickness, arching and graduation of the table are undoubtedly significant factors determining the response of the bass, and also in producing a quality sound. The table acts like the skin of a drum and vibrates in sympathy with the frequency of the string's vibration. This vibration is transmitted through the hard wood bridge supporting the strings, the feet of which are in contact with the table between the f holes. The body of the bass containing a large volume of air then acts as an amplifier. In general, the thinner the table the more responsive the bass and the louder the volume of sound produced. However, the stability of the bass and the prevention of cracks developing in the table, impose a limit to the amount of thinning which can be safely achieved.

The back and ribs of the bass are made from hardwood. Nicely figured maple is often the choice for top quality instruments. Sycamore, beech, poplar and pear wood have also been used. The back can either be flat which is easier to make (and should be cheaper too), or it can be carved to form an arched or swell back, often referred to as a 'round' back.

One of the most important and vital parts of a double bass is hidden from view, unless one looks through the f holes. This is the soundpost, a piece of wood of cylindrical form about 18mm in diameter. This is *'wedged'* between the table and the back on the treble side of the bass, a couple of centimetres or so below the foot of the bridge. Its exact placement and optimum position can only be determined by trial and error using a specialist tool called a soundpost setter. In my youthful ignorance I was unaware of this essential gadget but after many struggles and some colourful language, I managed to insert and set a soundpost using a large twin pronged meat fork! Incidentally, many years ago I came across a nice looking swell back bass in which the soundpost had been fixed permanently, using what appeared to be cascamite, an early resin glue. Presumably, some owner had slackened off the strings unaware that the soundpost is kept in position by the deformation of the table under string tension. He probably received a shock when the soundpost clattered down – a most alarming and depressing sound. Soundpost setting and its subsequent minute position adjustment, which has an immense effect on the bass's performance, are best left to a skilled bass luthier. Another vital but unseen part is the bass bar, a tapering piece of wood about 85 cm long on a ¾ bass, glued to the table on the bass side approximately under the foot of the bridge. This component, which cannot be adjusted, supports the table and also transmits vibrations over the full length of the table.

The hardwood neck of the bass with the scroll and pegbox at its upper end carries the ebony fingerboard, onto which the strings are pressed. The pegbox houses the required number of pegs around which one end of the string is wound. The pegs are operated by a worm and cog arrangement known as tuners. Due to the large string tension in general, ordinary violin/cello type pegs are unable to sufficiently tension the bass string. The mechanical advantage of the tuners achieves this with ease and tuners also have the advantage of precise tuning. After passing over the bridge the lower ends of the strings are secured into the ebony tailpiece, which is anchored to the endpin with a wire harness. The set-up is completed by an adjustable spike which passes through the endpin, individual players selecting the length of spike to suit their preference.

During the first few years of my close acquaintance with the double bass only one type of string was available. This was made of gut with the lower two strings spirally wound with thin wire. Gut strings were hard on the finger ends and from time to time inflicted much pain. The strings frayed easily, and the razor sharp slivers causing the anatomical trauma were best removed by running the flame from a cigarette lighter along the string to burn them off. Gut strings went out of tune quickly, particularly as the concert hall warmed up. Nylon strings were developed in an attempt to overcome these disadvantages but tonally in my experience, these were disappointing. However, gut strings have made something of a comeback for players attempting authenticity in period orchestras.

Modern strings are formed by spirally winding smooth steel around cores of various materials. These are much easier to play, light on the fingers and maintain pitch reasonably well. Strings are now available for specific types of playing, for example orchestral work where arco (bowing) dominates. Jazz players use strings specifically developed for pizzicato, whilst a compromise is available with so called hybrid strings. A range of tensions is also available, and this is really a preference choice depending on the type of playing and the characteristics of the bass. A set of the better quality steel strings is not cheap and because some make or type of string performs better on a particular bass, experimentation to find the optimum can be an expensive procedure.

Unlike other orchestral instruments in the string family which all have 4 strings, the bass is the exception. Over the course of several centuries basses have been made with 3, 4, 5 and even 6 strings. Throughout the 19th century and into the early 20th century the 3 string variety was very popular. A 3 string bass besides being more playable than one with 4 strings, exerts less pressure on the table and thus 'frees up' the sound. It is little wonder that Dragonetti (1763-1846) and Bottesini (1821-1889), the outstanding virtuosi of their respective eras, both played on 3 string basses. Indeed the 3 string bass was in use in England into the 1920's, up until the time that contracts for the London orchestras specified the 4 string instrument. The 3 string bass tuning was not standardised, but the most common seems to have been tuning in fourths, from the lowest sounding string A,d,g. The main alternative tuning was in fifths being G,d,a, which was Gilbert Pell's tuning of the dance band bass on which I originally learnt.

The tuning of 4 string basses which are the majority of instruments used presently, has been largely standardised to fourths tuning E,A,d,g. The advantage of this system is the ease with which octave intervals can be played without moving the hand position. A few players, notably the Canadians, Joel Quarrington and Max Kaspar, are using fifths tuning. The strings are tuned C,G,d,a, exactly one octave below the pitch of the cello. This tuning has the disadvantage of increasing the number of shifts (hand position changes) needed to execute a particular passage. The advantage is clearly that the range of the bass is enhanced, this being particularly desirable in the lower register in order to cope with much in the orchestral repertoire.

Many composers have written bass parts which have notes below that of the standard 4 string bass tuning, and instruments are currently being made and existing ones converted, to extend the compass downward by means of an extension. This is a narrow supplementary fingerboard extending along the scroll on the bass side of the instrument, and replacing the standard E string with a longer string tuned to C. The semitones between E and C are either achieved by simply fingering the string on the supplementary fingerboard, or by means of a mechanical device known as the Fawcett extension. In my experience the extension works best on long pedal notes and is less satisfactory in allegro passages, because the longer and slightly thicker C string does not 'speak' so readily.

Some players now prefer a 5 string bass to the 4 string with extension in order to obtain the lower notes. The lower fifth string is usually tuned to B, thus preserving the tuning in fourths across all strings. The slight disadvantage of the 5 string bass is that the finger board is wider and more difficult to get the hand around. Because the fifth string places an additional load on the table, the instrument has to be sturdier in construction which makes the instrument slightly heavier to carry around.

Certainly of paramount importance in orchestral playing is the bow, for it is this which controls the articulation and the dynamic. The shape of the bow has changed considerably over the centuries but by now two distinct types have emerged, each of which have their adherents. The two types are named German and French being indicative of the countries where they have developed.

In both cases the best sticks are made of Pernambuco wood and vary in length from about 63cm to about 73cm. In the case of a bass bow, the horse hair ribbon can either black or white according to player's choice. It is usually about 2 cm wide, and is fixed at the point of the bow with the other end attached to a 'frog', the position of which can be adjusted to tension the hair appropriately. The design of the *'frog'* is the major difference between the German and French style bows. In the former the *'frog'* is about 5 cm wide and in the latter about 3 cm wide. This width difference leads to two distinct bow holds. The German bow is gripped at the *'frog'* in an underhand position whilst the French bow is gripped in an overhand position similar to the hold for the violin, viola and cello bow. Traditionally the German bow has been dominant in central Europe, whilst the French pattern has been adopted in France and Britain, although today these preferences are breaking down.

12

The Bass - is it easy to play?

If I had £5 or even £1 every time I'd been asked this question about the bass, by now I'd be quite well off. As I remarked in an earlier chapter the simple answer is that there are no musical instruments which are easy to play, certainly none to a decent standard. Some are superficially easier in the sense that it is possible to produce a pleasing sound quite early in the practice process. For example the humble penny whistle, the recorder and any keyboard instrument, do not rely on the performer's skill to produce a sound which is immediately recognisable as characteristic of that instrument. In complete contrast, early efforts on any bowed string instrument are likely to disappoint, the sound produced being totally unlike the exquisite tone of the skilled performer.

Every instrument has its own particular difficulties which only relentless and dedicated hours of practice on a daily basis can overcome. Whatever the instrument, there are people out there in the wide world who are prepared to devote their lives to achieving complete mastery of their choice, and this level of attainment marks the standard for lesser mortals to aim at. Such superlative standards, in addition to being an inspiration are certainly a challenge, and believe me, are at times depressing.

The manifold difficulties of playing the bass stem entirely from its size, but even before attempting to play it there is the problem of transporting such a large, relatively heavy, and without doubt unwieldy, instrument. Most modern cars can be utilised as transport, the ideal being the estate type with a large rear opening tailgate and a flat floor to avoid having to lift the bass over a deep lip. In the years following the Second World War cars were often too small to accommodate the bass, and I remember one particular player who in all weathers, carried a rather nice English bass in a non-too waterproof cover strapped onto the car roof – looking back it hardly bears thinking about.

Having arrived in the vicinity of the venue there is then the problem of manhandling the instrument into the hall. Bass players are no more intrinsically punctual than any other orchestral members, however it is unusual to find them rushing in to a rehearsal at the last minute. There are no musical reasons for this apparent enthusiasm, simply the need to arrive early to grab a parking space nearby, thus avoiding a long tiring carry. It's no fun lugging an unwieldy mass the equivalent of almost two stones (13kg) of potatoes, together with a stool to sit on and often a music stand. Today all manner of gadgets ranging from single wheels to dual-purpose wheeled bass stools, have been devised to allow the bass to be trundled along. However, these mechanical devices cannot overcome the problem of a flight of stairs. Every bass player has at some time had to contend with this hazard. The ones with a narrow top step terminating with an outward opening spring loaded door are the ultimate nightmare! Many older bass players I have known have reluctantly ended their playing career not through lack of ability, but by being unable to cope with the problems of transportation and carrying. Incidentally, my sympathy goes out to harpists who have to cope with an even heavier instrument. What's more their troubles do not end once they are on stage as with so many strings, they then have to face a mammoth tuning task.

Turning now to actually playing the bass, as mentioned earlier every technical problem arises from size. It is of course essential to have a long heavy string to produce vibrations slow enough to provide the lowest pitch of the orchestra. The frequency of the lowest note, the E on a 4 string bass, is actually 41.20 Hz. 4 string basses with an extension produce a low C frequency of 32.70 Hz whilst on a 5 string bass the low B is vibrating at 30.87 Hz. The bass's vibrating string length (often referred to as the string stop) is around 106 cm give or take a cm or two. In contrast a violin's string stop is around 32 cm. The string diameter or gauge, which together with the material from which the string is made, determines the string's mass per unit length. This factor determines the pitch at a given string length and tension. In the case of a double bass the diameter of the lowest sounding string (on a 4 string bass the E string) is about 2.7mm whilst that of the lowest on the violin (the G string) is only 0.7mm. The string length and its mass make it difficult for the bow to start the bass string vibrating, when compared with other instruments of the bowed string family, especially the violin. The problem is particularly acute when attempting to play softly. The fact that the string does not react quickly can cause crisp articulation to be a rather hit and miss affair in fast musical passages.

Vibrations of the string are transmitted through the bridge to the bass's front, which effectively acts like the skin of a drum and causes the air inside the body to vibrate, along with the back and to a lesser extent the sides (ribs). On a ¾ size bass (the 'standard' orchestral size) the dimensions of the front are about 110cm in length, around 68cm at its widest and at its thickest some 10mm underneath the bridge. Corresponding measurements for a violin are 36cm, 21 cm and 2.6mm. Consideration of these dimensions inevitably leads to the conclusion that the front of a bass along with the back and ribs, requires far more energy to cause it to vibrate than that required on the smaller sized string instruments. The air inside the body also has mass and this has to commence vibrating. A bass contains roughly 80 times the volume of that in a violin, and it is no surprise that a bass is much slower to speak and difficult to articulate in fast passages.

The bow has a critical role in transmitting energy from the bowing arm to the string, and a bass bow is much heavier than one designed for the violin. My own French bow made by Jerome Thibouville-Lamy weighs 140 grams compared with a violin bow I own, which is 51 grams. The difference may not sound much, but the energy to reverse the momentum at the end of each stroke in a fast passage i.e. from a down bow to an up bow and vice versa is considerable, although after extensive practice is hardly noticeable. Due to the width of the bass and to a lesser extent the rib depth, there is a practical limit to the length of the bow which can be used effectively, particularly when playing on the string furthest from the bowing arm (the G string). It's simply another illustration of Sod's Law that the largest orchestral string instrument has the shortest bow. Consequently the musical phrase which can be sustained on the bass in one bow stroke in general, is shorter than other string instruments.

Throughout my bass playing career I've occasionally been frustrated by some of my bass section colleagues' obsession with copying the cello section's bowing for particular passages. Although I admit it does look nice to have both sections' bows moving in a synchronised manner, the practicalities of achieving that are sometimes not the most efficient way of bowing on the bass. Anyway, why should the basses copy the cellos, why not the other way around? With their longer bow and the ability to sustain a longer phrase it is easier for the cello to adapt to the bass bowing.

As a direct result of the long string stop on a bass, the fingering is far more difficult than on other instruments of the string family. In the first instance some greater finger pressure is needed to ensure a good clear sound. If that was not enough of a problem, the spacing of the fingers is such that in the lower two octaves of the range, the hand span between the index and fourth fingers of the left hand is just one tone. This means that only 3 major scales, the F, Bflat and G in the lower octave can be obtained without moving the hand to a new position – the hand movement being termed a shift. Every other major scale requires at least one shift. The extreme case occurs in ascending and descending the lower octave of the Fsharp major scale of six sharps (or the equivalent Gflat major scale of 6 flats) where no less than eight shifts are needed. In the case of the scales just mentioned, they are not played on a single string but by the bow crossing to an adjacent string at the appropriate note. String crossing on the bass is much more difficult than on other bowed string instruments, simply because the spacing between strings is that much wider – the bass approximately 26mm at the bridge compared with violin's 11mm. Of course it is possible to play scales on just one string, but on the bass massive shifts are needed. Taking the example of the ascending G major (1 sharp) scale played from the open G string (no fingers on the string), the hand has to move a distance of approximately 45cm, the exact figure depending on the actual string stop.

The fact that shifting is such an essential skill in bass playing, it is a technique which has to be constantly practiced for two specific reasons. First, to obtain sufficient speed to allow fast passages to be executed cleanly, and secondly to achieve good intonation. It is relatively easy to play in tune when all the notes are under the fingers, but once a shift is required it is a matter of venturing into the unknown. As a result of the wide spacing between the fingers poor intonation is not easily corrected, because one cannot roll the finger to achieve the correct pitch, a trick which can achieved on smaller string instruments.

Finally, it is worth noting that the bass is quite a physical instrument to play and a fair amount of strength is required, particularly in the fingers. For this reason, compared to other orchestral string instruments, prolonged practice periods on the bass are not possible – this excuse can be used to good effect by youngsters reluctant to practice!

13

Great Double Bass Myths

There's a story about the legendary violinist Fritz Kreisler visiting London in 1911. In a dealer's shop he was trying out a violin and was astonished by its beauty of tone, power and projection. He assumed the instrument to be by the Italian master Guarnari, considered by many to be the equal of Stradivari. He was so overwhelmed that he decided to purchase it there and then. When the dealer told him the violin was by Daniel Parker an 18th century English maker, Kreisler asked the dealer politely if he would oblige by removing the maker's label. He explained to the dealer that it wouldn't be the done thing for a world-renowned violinist of his standing to be seen playing an English violin. All credit to the dealer Hill, for refusing.

It's much the same with old basses. There are undoubtably many fine instruments by Italian makers such as Amati, Bergonzi, Montagnana, Testore, Gasparo da Salo, Storioni, Maggini, Gagliano, Ceruti and Grancino, but there are also superb basses by the leading English makers Lott, Tarr, Fendt, Cole, Kennedy, Hill, Taylor, Wamsley, Forster and others. Yet these latter instruments in general, are considered less desirable than their Italian counterparts and consequently less valuable. Naturally in the British bass world, English instruments are rated second to the Italians followed by German and French basses. Amongst the more desirable German basses are those by Klotz, Neuner, Bachman, Hildebrandt and Stainer – the latter although from Absam in the Austrian Tyrol, is always considered part of the German school of makers. From the French school Vuillaume, Gand, Quenoil, Barbe and Chanot are highly rated makers.

There is so much myth and mystique as well as snobbery that has developed over many years with regard to the superiority of Italian instruments, that good instruments by skilled makers from other countries are often dismissed. It does not follow that an old bass reputably by one of the best makers from whichever country, will necessarily play well, although the chances are that it will. Many years ago an opportunity arose for me to privately acquire a late 18th century bass by William Taylor. Despite its fine appearance and established provenance, as a player's instrument it was a sad disappointment and perhaps not typical of this maker. The thin, weak, 'wooden' tone, coupled with a slow response particularly in the lower register, did not make an attractive playing proposition. I've never been a collector of or investor in string instruments, so needless to say, I turned it down. On the other hand as a player, I have been pleasantly surprised by the attributes of several nondescript unlabelled specimens. The German 'Blockless Wonder' basses made in vast numbers of varying quality in Mittenwald and Markneukirchen, and imported quite cheaply into Britain from about the mid 19th to the early 20th centuries are a case in point. These instruments would never be collectors or investment pieces, yet from the playing point of view a few of the many I've tried over the years have been be very good indeed, and moreover light to carry around, particularly as one arrives at the veteran stage.

The attribution of a bass can increase enormously the value of the instrument, despite it playing exactly as did before the experts viewed it. That's really absurd and illogical, isn't it? It is also surprising how the experts' opinions can differ significantly. I remember with some affection a beautiful looking violin shaped bass with swell back and ribs of lovely figured maple, which I owned early in my career. Viewed from the front it bore a striking resemblance to the world renowned bass known as The Tarisio made between 1550 and 1560 by the Italian master Gasparo da Salo. My bass had been built originally as a 3 stringer which was later converted to 4 strings and it had no label or other brand to reveal even its country of origin, let alone its maker. In my youthful ignorance I was even beginning to believe it might have been made by da Salo. However I took it to be examined by three experts who each proposed a different country of origin, the only consensus was that it wasn't Italian! The bass possessed a very pleasing tone but sadly not much of it, and what I wanted in those days more than anything else was a loud instrument. I later came to regret selling it. Perhaps a tweak of the soundpost and proper setting up might have improved its performance no end, but then I was young and didn't know much about such matters.

On the question of value it is reckoned that the true value of a bass or for that matter any string instrument, is always found at a specialist auction where the knowledgeable market is the ultimate arbiter. I suppose this is true in the majority of cases, but anomalies are always possible and auction estimates are not always a reliable guide.

In June 2001 I sold a superb looking and fabulous sounding bass which I personally had attributed to Cole of Manchester. I consigned it to a fine musical instrument auction at one of the leading London auction houses. Some years earlier I had bought the bass in a dreadful state for £250. It was one of those rare lucky finds after I followed up advertisement in a Free Ads newspaper. Being a keen motorcyclist I could hardly believe my eyes. *'Swap or exchange old double bass with pickup, lovely tone for old motorcycle, preferably British 500cc+ but anything considered.'* After spending about £3,000 on a complete restoration the bass was rather too large for me to play comfortably, having a long string stop of 43.5 inches (110.5cm). I played it sporadically but eventually gave up the unequal struggle and I decided to send it to auction to achieve a quick hassle-free sale. The sale catalogue described the bass as *'A fine English four-stringed Bass probably by Cole of Manchester circa. 1880.'* The auction house expert had placed an estimate of £12,000 to £15,000 on the instrument. I had been hoping the bass might sell at the upper end of the range, if not for a shade more. In the event the bass realised £11,500 and in this case the estimate was pretty well spot on.

Fast forward to March 2010 and I was intrigued to see the instrument come up for sale again at the same auction house. The bass was now described in the catalogue as, *'An English Double Bass attributed to James Cole, Manchester 1880.'* This time the estimate had dropped to £8,000 to £10,000. Incredible as it may seem the bass realised £25,200! Way above the estimate - need I say more! I assume that there must have been at least two competing bidders who had both examined the bass carefully and been satisfied with its playing capability and its provenance. Auctions can indeed be unpredictable.

Amazingly the adventures of this bass were to continue, for sometime during the next three years it found its way across to the USA. As part of the stock of a well-respected string instrument dealership in Albuqueque, New Mexico, I found the bass illustrated and described on their website as, *'A fine bass by Cole of Manchester, 1880.'* The bass had by now acquired a fingered extension. The asking price was not specific, but listed at, *'over $50,000'* (approximately £35,000). It is interesting to note how the description had changed over the years from *'probably by'* (originally my term and accepted by the London auction house in 2001) and 'attributed' (London auction house second listing in 2010) to a firm attribution by the US string instrument dealer.

Although the experts have experience on their side, they rely to a large extent on stylistic characteristics and comparison with instruments of proven provenance in providing an attribution. However I'm not entirely convinced that the comparison technique would necessarily provide the correct answer in every case. Many string instrument makers must have experimented extensively throughout their careers searching for their ideal instrument pattern. Perhaps the most famous was Stradivari, who not only made innumerable trials of wood thickness and varnish, but also altered the designs of his violins in the 4 distinct periods now recognised in his long career. In the case of an instrument as large as the bass the urge to experiment is probably greater than that with smaller string instruments. In particular, the availability of suitable tone wood of large enough dimension must have been a factor in determining the size and outline of the bass in many cases.

A label inside the body of a string instrument is a notoriously unreliable guide to the instrument's maker, nevertheless many owners cling to the myth that their prize possession bearing a famous maker's label is the genuine article. For all manner of reasons over the centuries fake labels have been glued into copies of master instruments and, to a much lesser extent, genuine labels have been removed from authentic instruments and placed in inferior examples. The violin world provides the overwhelming case for treating labels with a huge dose of scepticism. Literally hundreds of thousands of copies of Stradivari violins have been made all over the world, many bearing a fake but apparently genuine label. Yet it is reckoned that Stradivari and his sons made around 1000 instruments of which approximately 600 have survived, representing but a tiny fraction of the number of copies. In the case of basses however there is much less likelihood of forgery than with violins, simply because they do not command such astronomical prices.

Over recent years the science of dendrochronology has finally come to assist in string instrument appraisal. Examination and measurement of the tree ring pattern found on the spruce wood of the belly of the instrument can be compared with reference chronologies from particular areas where these trees are grown, and thus provide a possible date for when the spruce tree was felled. The date of the latest tree ring found on the belly is therefore the earliest date that the instrument could possibly have been made. In practice it is likely to have been several years after that date to allow time for the wood to mature. It is also likely that some of the youngest outer tree rings have been lost in preparing the wood ready for carving.

With sensational results, the dendrochronology technique has been used to date the spruce wood used in the construction of one of the world's most famous basses – The Karr-Koussevitzky. This bass, a favourite of the bass virtuoso and conductor Serge Koussevitzky was widely believed to have been made by the Amati brothers Antonio and Girolamo in 1611. If authentic the bass would be the only known example by these brothers. Koussevitsky purchased the instrument in France in the early years of the 20th century, although nothing was known of its provenance. Some 11 years after his death in 1951, his widow Olga attended the debut recital of the bass virtuoso Gary Karr and was so overwhelmed by the experience she presented him with her late husband's favourite bass. In 2004 Karr then donated this instrument to the International Society of Bassists. In 2005 the result of tree ring dating of the instrument was published. The belly of the bass contained a remarkable 317 year tree ring record dating from 1445 to 1761. Unequivocally, this evidence shows that the bass could not have been made by the Amati brothers in the early 17th century, for the last tree ring of 1761 is some 150 years later than the supposed date of construction, and over 100 years after the death of Antonio, the last of the brothers to die. The tree ring date is also a clear indication of the fallibility associated with stylistic attribution of string instruments generally, not just of this particular instrument. A timely warning to the experts! This bass is an unusual viola da gamba pattern, and this particular feature had been taken by some authorities to represent the earlier form of viol but modified by the Amatis. Furthermore it was argued that this form then became standard in the late 17th and 18th centuries. To add to the uncertainty it had also been pointed out that the shape closely resembled that favoured by Stradivari for a viola da gamba, in particular the form of the f holes. Antonio Stradivari died in 1737 and his sons Omobono and Francesco in 1742 and 1743 respectively. Quite clearly this bass could not have been made in the Stradivari workshop either, although the later unknown maker may well have been influenced by Stradivari's work. Science destroys another myth!

Perhaps the greatest myth of all is that modern basses made by present-day master craftsmen cannot match up to those made by the old masters. In terms of the workmanship this is simply not true. However, what matters most to a player is how well the bass plays. As far as I am aware, there have been no blind trials comparing the sound of modern basses with that of old instruments. Many trials comparing old master violins with quality hand crafted instruments of contemporary makers have invariably produced an identical conclusion. Quite simply the judges were unable to distinguish between the two categories. I suspect the same would be true in a blind bass trial. That does not mean all basses would produce an identical sound. Quite the contrary, some would produce a bright sound, others a sweeter mellower tone, some would be capable of giving a massive loud sound, others a softer more refined tone. Each would have its own characteristics and much is down to player preference.

Stars of the Bass Firmament

Ask any group of music lovers to name a few virtuosi violinists and they'll reel off a list probably containing Maxim Vengerov and Nigel Kennedy from the modern era, whilst names such as Isaac Stern (1920-2001), Yehudi Menuhin (1916-99), Jascha Heifetz (1901-87), Fritz Kreisler (1875-1962), Joseph Joachim (1831-1907) and Niccolo Paganini (1782-1840) would feature from earlier times. That same group would also be able to list virtuosi pianists, cellists and possibly recall the internationally renowned violists Lionel Tertis (1876-1975) and William Primrose (1904-82). However it's almost certain that there would be blank looks all round if asked to name just one bass virtuoso.

The reason is not difficult to find. The bass is rarely let out of captivity from the confines of the orchestra to perform in a solo role. Although there are now many CD recordings of bass concertos and other solo works, I can only ever remember attending two orchestral concerts where the double bass was the featured solo instrument. The first occasion was in the early 1970's, when Peter Leah of the Halle Orchestra and later principal bass of the BBC Northern Orchestra was the soloist. More recently, in 2014, Tyler Shepperd, principal bass of the Welsh Nation Opera, gave a superb performance of the Bottesini concerto in Cardiff.

Throughout the centuries there have been many bass players who have made outstanding contributions to the art of playing the instrument either, through their individual performances or through teaching, the latter often leaving a legacy of instruction books, tutors and studies. Although there may have been others whose names have been lost in the mists of time, one of the earliest stars must have been Jan Zelenka (1679-1745) born in what is now the Czech

Republic. He was a bass player in the Dresden court of Augustus, Elector of Saxony, and there he also achieved fame as the Court Composer. If he had not been a successful baroque composer perhaps his name would be unknown today.

From about the middle of the 18th century and for the next hundred years Vienna achieved pre-eminence in music, and it was to this city that many of the finest bass players gravitated. Collectively this group of virtuosi are known today as the Vienesse School. Amongst them Joseph Kaempfer (1735-c1800), Friedrich Pichelberger (1741-1813), Johann Matthias Sperger (1750-1812) and Johann Hindle (1792-1861) were leading exponents. In a bass playing context, this period is often referred to as the golden age of virtuosity.

It is hardly surprising therefore that this period also saw the composition of many of the famous and some of the most difficult bass concertos. Works by Karl Kohaut (1726-1784), Johann Baptist Vanhal (1739-1812), Karl Ditters von Dittersdorf (1739-1799), Antonio Capuzzi (1753-1818), Domenico Dragonetti (1763-1846) and Giovanni Battista Cimador (1761-1805) still feature in today's bass soloist's repertoire, and are often requested in professional orchestral auditions as well as being set pieces in higher grade examinations.

Developing in parallel with the Viennese School was the Prague School founded by Wenzeslas Hause (1764-1845) which was centred at the Conservatory in that city. Hause's pupil Josef Hrabe (1816-1870) has left his mark on the profession through his Practical Tutor and 2 books of Etudes which were first edited by his pupil Franz Simandl (1840-1912), and then by Fred Zimmermann (1906-1967) a later descendent of the Prague School. The publications by Hrabe and Simandl's 2 volume New Method for the Double Bass have been outstanding and stood the test of time, still being in print to the present day. Many generations of bass students developed a love/hate relationship with these works but most with hindsight, have fond memories of mastering at least some of the exercises. Simandl must also take credit for standardising the fingering system using the 1st, 2nd and 4th fingers of the left hand for notes in the lower octave of each string. The vast majority of today's players use this system. Two later members of the Prague School, Frantisek Posta (1919-1991) who was principal bass in the Czech Philharmonic for over 40 years, and Ludwig Streicher (1920-2003) principal bass in the Vienna Philharmonic for some 19 years, have made significant contributions to modern bass technique. As well as their orchestral commitments both were pedagogues and soloists. Streicher also published a 3 volume method My Way of Playing Double Bass.

Prominent in the French school of bassists were Achille Gouffe (1804-1874) and Edouard Nanny (1872-1942). By all accounts both were brilliant artists on the instrument. Referring to Gouffe, no less an authority than Berlioz described him as a master virtuoso. In the 19th century Gouffe was one of the first to adopt the 4 string bass in France, and in 1839 wrote one of the first methods Traite sur la Contra-Basse a quatre cordes for this set up. He also published 45 Etudes and wrote many individual works for the solo bass. Nanny is perhaps best remembered for his Methode Complete pour la Contrabasse a quatre et cinq cordes, a unique work of 1920, since it dealt with the 5 string bass at a time when the 3 string bass was still in widespread orchestral use.

In the modern era Claude Hobday (1872-1954), Eugene Cruft (1887-1976), Gerald Drucker (1925-2010), Francois Rabbath, Franco Petracchi, Rinat Abragimov, Thomas Martin, Rodney Slatford and David Hayes have all raised the profile of the instrument and contributed significantly to the development of bass technique. Their involvement has embraced a wide range of activities as soloists, pedagogues, and in masterclasses and workshops, as well as commissioning new works and publishing a wide range of bass repertoire.

Missing from the list so far are four players who I believe represent the pinnacle of performance in their respective eras, from the mid 18th century to the present day. They are in chronological order Domenico Dragonetti (1763-1846), Giovanni Bottesini (1821-1889), Serge Koussevitzky (1874-1951) and Gary Karr (b 1941).

Domenico Carlo Maria Dragonetti, referred to by contemporaries as Il Drago was a truly remarkable character, some would say an extreme eccentric. He was an avid collector not only of musical instruments but of paintings, snuff boxes and remarkably, dolls. It is certain that he was not born into a privileged Viennese family but was the son of a barber, who also happened to play the guitar and the bass. Initially Dragonetti played the guitar but secretly practiced on his father's bass. At the age of 12 he received lessons from Michele Berini who was a bass player at the theatre, and also a member of the orchestra of the Ducal Chapel of San Marco. The young Dragonetti clearly had an outstanding aptitude for the instrument for, after 11 lessons Berini declared that he could teach him nothing further. A year later he was engaged as principal bass at Venice's Opera Buffa. In 1784 aged 21 he failed his first audition to win a position in the Ducal Chapel orchestra, but a second attempt 3 years later saw him appointed as the fifth of five basses. His undoubted talent soon saw him promoted to principal bass. His fame spread throughout Europe and the Russian Court attempted to lure him away with a tempting offer. The Chapel authorities were keen to retain his services and declined on his behalf, awarding him a huge salary increase to make his stay truly worthwhile.

In 1794 he moved to London initially on a 2 year leave of absence from San Marco, which the authorities later extended by a further 3 years. His friend the composer Giovanni Battista Cimador (1761-1805) who had already made a name for himself in London, encouraged him to make the move. Cimador composed a Concerto in G presumably for Dragonetti, whilst both men were still in Venice. The slow movement of this work is one of the most melodic and beautiful pieces for the solo bass.

A scholarly book by Fiona M Palmer, *'Domenico Dragonetti in England (1794-1846): the career of a double bass virtuoso, OUP 1997'*, which resulted from her thorough original research, provides a fascinating account of his life and far reaching musical influence in his adopted country. Although on several occasions he returned to Venice for short periods, he remained a towering figure not only as bass virtuoso, but also in the entire English orchestral music scene until his death in 1846.

In England Dragonetti initially was engaged to play at the King's Theatre, the home of Italian Opera, where he was desk partner of the celebrated Yorkshire cellist, Robert Lindley. This partnership lasted for an incredible 52 years. Additional orchestral involvement in London included membership of the Philharmonic Society Orchestra and the Ancient Concerts, the latter founded to promote early composers' work. In other public and private concerts throughout England he astounded and amazed the audience with his solo performances. Out of the London season he and Lindley travelled to the provinces, fashionable Bath in particular, where they took part in music festivals of all descriptions. Not only could he count members of the aristocracy amongst his friends but also the composers Haydn, Beethoven, Cimador, and also the founder of the music publishing house Vincent Novello. He became the highest paid orchestral musician in Britain, and by the time of his death he had amassed considerable wealth and a fabulous collection of basses. As a composer himself, he wrote a great many solos for the double bass including concertos, but recently it has been suggested his concerto in G is actually the work of Edouard Nanny. His favourite instrument was a 3 string bass by Gasparo de Salo (1542-1609) reputed to have been given to him by the Benedictine Nuns in the town of Vicenza where he had an engagement at the Grand Opera. He used a short bow with an outward curving stick very similar to one from a child's bow and arrow set. Using such a primitive bow and with the bass set up with gut strings high above the fingerboard for extra power, this must have been a challenge to his stamina and made articulation in fast passages extremely difficult. The fact that he was able to achieve this shows the strength in his left hand and fingers. It is a testament to the long hours of practice often far into the night, he was said to have done in his younger days. It is interesting to also note that he developed his own fingering system involving his thumb and all four digits.

How did the contemporaries of Dragoneti view his achievements and character? The obituary in The Musical World of 9th May 1846 gives us an insight:

> Dragonetti was not only the greatest performer of his age on the double bass - possessing the finest instinct of true excellence in all that concerns his art - but he had moral qualities of a high order; a benevolent and generous disposition, and an inclination to friendship, which he exercised with judgment and discrimination in men and things.

The outstanding bass virtuoso of the next generation was Giovanni Bottesini and although he would have been aged 25 when Dragonetti died it is not known whether the two met. The nickname given to Bottesini by his contemporaries, Paganini of the Double Bass, surely affirms his remarkable bass playing talents. Not only did he compose and play some of the most difficult pieces in the bass repertoire (some of which are seldom played today because of that fact), but it was the exquisite manner in which he performed. Bottesini however was not a one trick pony and his musical achievements and influence spread over a much wider spectrum. He achieved great success as an opera composer and as a conductor. Of interest to opera lovers is the fact that he conducted the first performance of Verdi's Aida in 1871.

He was born in 1821 into a musical family, the sixth of eight siblings at Crema, Lombardy. His father was an accomplished amateur clarinettist and composer, and it was from him that he received his first music theory lessons. His early musical experiences were wide, for even before the age of 11 he had sung in choirs, played the tympani in the cathedral orchestra and had already absorbed 6 years of violin lessons from a family friend Carlo Cogliati. His father entertained musical ambitions for him and in 1835 applied on his behalf for a place at the Milan Conservatory. There were only two scholarships remaining, one for bassoon the other for double bass. Presumably because of his knowledge of string instruments he chose the latter, but he had only a very short time to prepare for the audition. During the course of the audition he realised he was dreadfully out of tune so he stopped playing and addressed the panel, *"I hear gentlemen that I am out of tune, but when I know where to put my fingers I shall play out of tune no more"* – or so the story goes. Whatever the truth, the adjudicating panel was clearly impressed with his potential and offered him the place to study under Professor Luigi Rossi.

He made outstanding progress in his conservatory studies such that the governors allowed him to graduate early (in 1839) and presented him with a gift of 300 lire, which he put towards purchasing a bass. He made a fortunate find of a superb instrument which had been made in 1716 by the Milanese luthier Carlo Antonio Testore. The circumstance of its discovery is remarkable. The bass had apparently been abandoned in a marionette theatre when the previous owner Fiandro had died. He received a tip-off from bassist Arpesani and the two of them found it in a very distressed condition under a pile of old clothes. Bottesini fitted it up, converted it from a 4 stringer to a 3 stringer and this fabulous bass remained his faithful companion throughout his long career. When the English bassist Claude Hobday acquired it in 1898 the bass was converted back to 4 strings.

Unlike Dragonetti who never toured after he left Italy, Bottesini performed extensively throughout the western world. He commenced his solo career in his home city Crema in 1840, and for the next 6 years had many solo engagements in Italy and Austria. However, whilst principal bass at the La Fenice theatre Venice he met Verdi, and the two men became lifelong friends. His first overseas foray in 1846 found him in Havana where in addition to being the leading bassist, it saw him conduct the premiere of his first opera composition Cristoforo Colombo.

His first of many appearances in England was in 1849 when he played several solos at John Ella's Musical Union. An accurate assessment of his sheer virtuosity is given in a contemporary account of the performance:

> How he bewildered us by playing all sorts of melodies, as though he had a hundred nightingales caged in his double bass. Where he got his harmonic sequences from; how he swarmed up and down the fingerboard.......how his bow moved with the rapidity of lightening.....I never wearied of his consummate grace and finish, his fatal precision, his heavenly tone, his fine taste. One sometimes yearned for a touch of human imperfection, but he was like a dead shot, he never missed what he aimed at, and he never aimed at less than perfection.

His enormous work ethic saw him conducting operas in many major cities, his major triumph being the first performance of Verdi's Aida which was met with universal acclaim. However, he never abandoned the solo bass career and during the intermissions of opera performances he was conducting, he would even bring his bass on stage and entertain the audience, often with his fantasias on operatic themes.

Remarkable though Bottesini was as a composer, with over 30 bass solos, a tutor book, 13 complete operas, and a host of miscellaneous works which together with his undoubted talent as a conductor, it is for his virtuosic bass playing that he is remembered today. Without doubt he raised the standard of performance on the instrument, and he continued performing up to the time of his death in Parma in 1889. His obituary in the Musical Times provides a fitting tribute his prowess:

> On his favourite instrument, the double bass, he was absolutely phenomenal. The beauty of tone and sound he elicited from that unwieldy instrument, his marvellous facility, not to say agility, in executing the most difficult passages – the grace, elegance, and delicacy of his touch and method, gave proof of the most consummate and unrivalled talent. ......In precision, dash, accuracy, and in softness of touch and phrasing, Bottesini had no equal on the contra-basso.

In complete contrast to Bottesini, Serge Koussevitsky, although a hero amongst bass players, is remembered by the music loving public today as a successful conductor. Perhaps this is mainly because he abandoned his solo career for the last 23 years of his life to concentrate on conducting and other musical interests – another contrast to Bottesini who carried on playing until his death.

Koussevitsky was born in 1874 into a musical family in Kallinin some 100 miles northwest of Moscow. From an early age he played an assortment of instruments including the viola, cello, piano, and trumpet, and he received his first double bass lesson at the age of 13. He gained his early orchestral experience under his father, who directed a small amateur ensemble. At the age of 14, with a view to him becoming a conductor, he was keen to study music theory and composition at Moscow's Philharmonic Music School. His father unfortunately raised strong objections to him following this course and placed many obstacles in his path. The solution Koussevitsky adopted was a bold and daring one and an indication of his determination. He simply ran away from home! A double bass scholarship allowed him to study with Professor Joseph Rambousek (1845-1901) and in so doing became a 4th generation descendent of the Prague School. He worked assiduously at perfecting his technique and by the age of 16 while still a student, he had developed a successful soloist's career. Shortly afterwards he was appointed principal bass of the Imperial Orchestra. In 1894 he graduated and joined the bass section of the Bolshoi Theatre orchestra as well as continuing as a soloist, performing in most European Countries.

A second marriage in 1905 to Natalya Ushkova the daughter of a wealthy merchant, allowed him to develop his musical career in other directions. He founded a music publishing house through which he promoted the works of fellow Russian composers including Scriabin, Prokofiev and Rachmaninov. In 1909 further finance from his wife's family allowed him to establish a private orchestra which toured widely throughout Russia, and provided him with valuable conducting experience. His conducting prowess was such that by 1917 he was appointed director of the Russian State Symphony Orchestra, and in 1918 Moscow's Grand Opera. Unsurprisingly with his recent background and connections he did not find favour with the new rulers of Russia after the Revolution, who prevented him leaving the country. However in 1920 he was granted a year's leave of absence, so he took the opportunity to settle in Paris, where he continued his conducting career alongside his bass recitals.

1924 was a momentous year for Koussivitsky for it was then that he accepted an invitation to become permanent conductor of the renowned Boston Symphony Orchestra, a position he retained until 1949, some 2 years before his death. It was during this period that he was at his most productive commissioning many major orchestral works, conducting outstanding premieres, and drawing the world's attention to American composers. By the late 1920's his exhausting schedule caused him to terminate his career as a solo recitalist, but not before he had recorded for posterity his truly outstanding talent on the double bass. Those recordings together with his many compositions for solo bass are his legacy to the double bass fraternity.,

It is interesting to look back and read what the critics thought of his solo playing. The Morning Post review of his first London recital in 1907 compared him favourably with Bottesini:

> Nearly 18 years have passed since Giovanni Bottesini died, and until the present day no one has come forward to lay claim to the unique position which he held as a soloist upon the double bass. Mr Sergei Kussevitsky, who made his first appearance in this country as a double bass soloist yesterday at Bechstein Hall, may well be hailed as Bottesini's successor. He produces the same sweet tone - if anything, a little fuller - and has great command of the extensive fingerboard. To describe the instrument as unwieldy is unfair, in view of the manner in which it is handled by this executant.

Moving finally to the modern era, Gary Karr was born in Los Angeles in 1941 and has the distinction of being the first to make a career entirely as a solo bassist. The fact that he chose this instrument at a young age is no surprise since he is descended from a long line of bassists. His teachers included Warren Benfield, Stuart Sankey and Hermann Reinshagen, the latter being a 5th generation descendent of the Prague School. The public's attention was drawn to him in 1962 when he appeared as soloist playing The Swan from Saint-Saens Carnival of the Animals in a New York Philharmonic Young People's Concert conducted by Leonard Bernstein. This was broadcast on national television and later on international television.

That same year he made his recital debut at New York Town Hall and it was on this occasion that Koussivitsky's widow Olga was in the audience. She was so moved by his performance and convinced the spirit of her late husband was present, that she presented him with his 'Amati' bass. He became concerned regarding the future of this instrument and was determined that it should not be sold for profit, but passed to another player. To this end in 1984 he set up the Karr Doublebass Foundation also with the aim of acquiring fine instruments to lend to talented bassists. To promote the study and advancement of the bass and also to raise its profile in 1967 he founded the International Institute for the String Bass, the fore-runner of the International Society of Bassists (ISB). The 'Amati' bass, often now referred to as the Karr-Koussivitsky bass, he donated to the ISB in 2005.

From the time of his debut as a soloist, travel by air allowed him to make extensive world-wide tours, which had been impossible for virtuosi from earlier generations. By undertaking such extensive travel he was able to reach live audiences in countries which had previously been denied the stimulus of hearing virtuosi bassists. In this respect he has achieved two major objectives: first that of raising the profile of the bass amongst the concert going public, and second, inspiring and raising the level of proficiency amongst bassists.

He is renowned as a teacher, having held positions at the Julliard, Yale University and several other establishments in America and Canada. The interviews he has given indicate a real love of this mysterious art of teaching, the following being typical of his approach:

"I am not one of those teachers who desire the students to copy them. Every student is different and their special talents are not all the same. I want my students to learn to be independent of me but I want to share with them the skills that are required to accomplish a lot in the practice room. If I have succeeded in teaching my students how to practice I will feel very satisfied."

He has been keen to encourage children as young as eight to take up the instrument and to this end has produced a unique set of tutor books. Although he plays with a German style bow, he insists his students learn both the German and French bows as he believes that by so doing their appreciation of the merits of each will enhance their technique. His radical and experimental approach to the bass extends to the tuning, and he is an advocate of a 'hybrid' system. He advocates a fifth tuning between the lower three strings and a fourth tuning between the upper two strings resulting in a tuning of CGdg, thus increasing the downward compass.

Gary Karr's solo repertoire is extensive, ranging from concertos of the classical period to modern works, many of which he has commissioned, as well as transcriptions of other instrumental repertoire. Having lived through a period when instrumental recording has undergone profound advancement, one of his legacies will be the vast library of recordings which he has left for posterity, appreciated not only by bassists but by music lovers worldwide.

In the 1980's I had the privilege of hearing him perform a recital at Howell's School in Cardiff. I had heard him on record and seen him perform on television and therefore I had a good idea what to expect in the technical sense – nothing less than perfection. What was entirely unexpected was the enthusiasm and shear fun he derived in his playing, which was transmitted to a tremendously appreciative audience. If I was asked to pick out one technical aspect of this performance I would choose the beautiful full rich tone and perfect articulation throughout the instrument's compass. I can still hear that sound some 30 years later!

15

Gallery

Bamford Hoyle
– my mentor with 1800 Ceruti Bass

Gentlemen of Jazz
– Trad sounds of the 1950's

Back Row from left, Edward Hellewell (trombone),
ordon Beaumont (drums), John Hallas (cornet), Ian Ellis (tenor sax

Front Row from left, Phillip Tatchell (banjo),
Garth Hutchinson (clarinet), Richard Haigh (piano).

Clayton West Brass Band
1952

In uniform of Skelmanthorpe Band
1953

Off to give a solo performance
1955

Huddersfield Philharmonic Orchestra
1961

'Cole' Bass
London auction house catalogue 2001

Bass by Mike Hart commissioned 2010
4 string bass, violin shape with low C extension
Edward with Mike

Edward G Hellewell with Hungarian 5 string bass
2016

CPO bass section on stage St.David's Hall
Cardiff 2012

CPO on stage St. David's Hall
Cardiff 2012

Design & Print by AA Media Print Management Ltd.
www.aamedia.co.uk